HAMLET'S DIV

Hamlet's Divinity

AND OTHER ESSAYS

CHRISTOPHER DEVLIN

with an introduction by
C. V. WEDGWOOD

Essay Index Reprint Series

 BOOKS FOR LIBRARIES PRESS
FREEPORT, NEW YORK

#121408

Copyright © 1963 Madeleine Devlin

Reprinted 1970 by arrangement with
Rupert Hart-Davis Limited

INTERNATIONAL STANDARD BOOK NUMBER:
0-8369-1915-7

LIBRARY OF CONGRESS CATALOG CARD NUMBER:
77-128234

PRINTED IN THE UNITED STATES OF AMERICA

Contents

Introduction

BY

C. V. WEDGWOOD

CHRISTOPHER DEVLIN died on 5 October 1961 at the age of fifty-four. He had entered the Society of Jesus in 1926 and was ordained priest in 1938. During the War he served as a Chaplain in the R.A.F., at first in England at Tangmere, later in West Africa, the Middle East and Italy. Some years after the War he went back to Africa as a missionary priest and remained there until his serious illness compelled him to return to England in 1959.

Although he had some quieter years of teaching and writing between the end of the war and his departure for the mission field, much of his life was devoted to active, exacting and sometimes dangerous work. Such time as he had to give to the literary and historical questions which interested him so deeply, he used as fully as possible. He was a frequent contributor to *The Month*. He wrote—it was the fruit of seven years' study and research—a biography of *Robert Southwell, Poet and Martyr*, which was published in 1956. Three years later appeared his authoritative edition of *The Sermons and Devotional Writings* of Gerard Manley Hopkins. In the last eighteen months of his life, though very ill, he completed a study of the character and writings of Christopher Smart, *Poor Kit Smart*, which was published shortly before his death.

Although the historical and literary interests which I shared with him might well have brought me into touch with him as a fellow-worker in the same field, our friendship in fact began at a much earlier date and before either of us had published anything. In February 1932 one of my closest

6

childhood friends, Madeleine Oppenheimer, married his brother Patrick, and it was at their wedding that I first met Christopher.

He was very young then, but already he seemed to have some spiritual quality that set him apart. Whether his features were grave or were transformed by his sudden enchanting smile, one noticed at once the gentleness of his expression, but a gentleness that suggested strength. Here, one felt, was a dedicated man. I saw him first in the half-light of the church during the wedding ceremony and noticed—without then knowing who he was—the young serious face with the keen eyes and the high cheek-bones and the withdrawn unworldly quality of his expression. Only when we came out afterwards into the sunlight, and introductions were made, did I realise that he was in truth a dedicated man. He had already found his vocation and was a Scholastic at Heythrop.

It needed only a few moments of conversation to reveal his exceptional intelligence, but his was an intelligence that, all his life, he carried and used with humility. One felt that he had no need of Donne's prayer for help against the over-confidence of the intellectual:

> That learning, Thine ambassador,
> From Thine allegiance we never tempt.

Almost every time that I met him he was with his family. It was at the home of Patrick and Madeleine that I got to know him. At first I would meet him with them, later with them and their children. When I call up his picture it is always in this setting—casual, friendly, informal, with the children playing round about or, as they grew older, joining in the talk.

Such a setting must, of course, give only a very partial impression of one whose life was dedicated to a greater service than that of home and kindred. None the less, these memories preserve for me a visual image of his qualities—his gaiety, tenderness and love, and his essential simplicity of spirit.

We talked a great deal about history and about literature.

7

His firm and gentle voice, his courtesy, his humour and his clarity of mind made our discussions a delight. His learning was wide and he had a persuasive power of marshalling his arguments, but I never remember his forcing an opinion or going out of his way to score a point. We were not always in agreement. We started, after all, from widely dissimilar points of view. Both of us, as historians, were concerned with the ferocious century of the Counter-reformation (I in its latter half and he in its earlier stages), and my own roots are deep in the Puritan-Protestant tradition. But our discussions were always friendly and always to me refreshing and illuminating.

The essays in this book range freely over literature and history but all alike deal with this epoch. Even Shakespeare, although his transcendant genius is timeless, was a man of the Counter-reformation. We are apt to forget, in the insular textbook view of English history, that the end of Elizabeth's reign and the early Stuart period fall within this long age of international violence and religious conflict. England was part of a Christendom divided into two worlds, mutually fearing and threatening each other; it was a time of permanent cold war, varied at frequent intervals by shooting wars of exceptional bitterness.

The adoption of the Catholic Crusade by the Spanish-Austrian Habsburg dynasty intensified a dangerous confusion of religious and political elements. Religion was made to play a dominant part in the ruthless power-politics of rising monarchies or emergent national states. In the interests of their faith, or their countries, the leaders on both sides were forced into ruthless and devious actions. On both sides evil elements came to the top, and the finest and most sensitive spirits were often corrupted or destroyed, or fell victims to force. The corruption of character and the waste of virtue is, humanly speaking, the most tragic aspect of such epochs of irreconcilable division.

This tragedy of waste and deterioration was something that Christopher Devlin felt very deeply. His sense of it is always present in the background of his writing on this epoch, even when he is writing of lesser things, or exercising his ingenious talent for historical detection. The secrecy and complexity that naturally attend a time of war and espionage have left many mysteries and many dark places in the history of this period. The last years of Elizabeth and the first years of James I are full of enigmas in relation to the English Roman Catholic minority. On some of these Father Devlin exercised an unusual and patient skill which make his elucidations fascinating to follow, as he deftly singles out the clues and unravels the tangled evidence.

His approach was always generous, chivalrous even, with a touch of the romantic. Sometimes he practised what might almost be called a knight-errantry of scholarship, a setting out to rescue something or someone obscured, traduced, forgotten. His last published book, a sympathetic and deeply understanding study of Christopher Smart has a strong element of this. It was not merely a voyage of discovery into some of the dark places of the eighteenth century and the abysses of the human spirit, it was a quest to regain the truth and to re-establish the human worth and human dignity of poor Kit Smart.

But what, to my mind, distinguishes Christopher Devlin's writing and thinking is above all a radiant compassion—a compassion which lit up and gave dignity sometimes to the obscurest and most unlikely people. Most historians (unless they are exclusively devoted to a theoretical or statistical approach) know what it is to feel sympathy or pity or affection for the characters who come under their scrutiny. I would be the last to deny that such feelings, when linked to disciplined scholarship, can be of real value. But they can also degenerate into a facile and self-indulgent function of the imagination: it is so easy to feel a vague and amiable pity for the misfortunes of those who are safely dead and on whose behalf we have no need to exert ourselves.

On re-reading these essays I have been struck again and again by the *active* quality of Christopher Devlin's imagination. For him everyone of whom he wrote was an immortal soul, a man made in the image of God. This I believe is the secret of his convincing treatment of human character, so that we become deeply concerned about, for instance, the identity and fate of Christopher Blount, or feel distress for the

9

vigorous young Earl of Derby (Shakespeare's patron) struck down so prematurely—though not by witchcraft.

This quality of compassionate understanding is perhaps most clearly illustrated in his treatment of so slight and minor a figure as the unfortunate Hesketh hanged for treason at St Albans in 1593. Putting together the fragmentary evidence about his life in exile abroad, his return, his voyage to his native North country, his letters to his wife, Father Devlin creates a slight but real figure, and when the hideous Kafka-like predicament closes in on the wretched man, with his arrest and trial for treason, we feel the horror of it. Here is not just another expendable victim of high statecraft, but a living man who suffered. Father Devlin, by a legitimate exercise of the imagination, has allowed one beam of light and consolation to fall on his ghastly death. In this passage it seems to me that the poet in Christopher Devlin enabled him to do something more than the merely historical. Whether or not we accept his reconstruction of what happened to the luckless Hesketh, the story as he tells it has the true quality of pity and terror that we associate with tragedy.

Some of these essays throw light on obscure by-ways of our history, some will suggest clues and questions to other students of the period, some will provoke argument. All are interesting, alive, and wrought with a craftsman's feeling for the language and a scholar's love of his subject.

Shakespeare's Faith

SHAKESPEARE—though the fact is not generally known—was seriously accused in his life-time of being a pro-Catholic propagandist. I want to treat of his Catholicism by exploring the background of this accusation, rather than by encroaching on his poetic genius which is something quite apart from religious controversy.

In the first place let us settle once and for all the matter of Shakespeare's religious upbringing. It is quite certain that his childhood and his boyhood were passed in a family atmosphere that was devoutly Catholic—not just vaguely Catholic, as is often supposed, but definitely "Recusant." The main evidence for this—to which I have some additions to make—was provided more than half a century ago by two Catholic scholars, Richard Simpson and Fr Herbert Thurston. Their findings, however, made little impression on biographers of Shakespeare, until quite recently—in 1946—a book appeared by an American, Mr de Wulf, called *The Shakespeares and the Old Faith*. In this book there was nothing of importance which had not already been put forward by Simpson or by Thurston; but the fact that it issued from a neutral academic source in a more or less definitive manner must now oblige us to take account of what has hitherto been so oddly neglected.

The evidence is briefly as follows. John Shakespeare, William's father, though of country stock, became a flourishing citizen of Stratford during Queen Mary's reign and the first years of Elizabeth's. He rose to be a magistrate and an Alderman, and was entitled to a coat of arms and to call himself a gentleman. Then, from about 1575 onwards, he suffered increasingly from financial embarrassment, until in 1592 he is found refusing to come to the Parish Church for fear of being arrested for debt. Hitherto the supposition had been that, having proved himself an excellent business-man up to middle age, he then abruptly changed his habits and became a spendthrift. Richard Simpson however, was aware that "fear of being arrested for debt" as an excuse for not coming to the Protestant church, was an accepted euphuism in the case of recusants who were still locally popular and respected. (Simpson, I may say, beside being deeply versed in recusant history, was a distinguished Shakespearean scholar in his own right: he was the first person to detect the hand of Shakespeare in the play *Sir Thomas More*.) Simpson, then, discovered that the 1592 list which contained John Shakespeare's name was nothing else but a list of Catholics who were Recusants, i.e. who consistently refused to attend Protestant worship; the list contained well-known Catholic names such as Arden, Middlemore and Catesby and Throckmorton, and incidentally two names of Stratford citizens which are of interest as figuring shortly afterwards in William Shakespeare's History Plays—namely Bardolph and Fluellen! Simpson used this and other arguments to show that consistent Recusancy, not extravagance, was the cause of John Shakespeare's financial troubles, such as the conveyance to come,[1] beginning as they did in the 1570s when the pressure

[1] ". . . the withdrawal from public life, once vaguely believed to be . . . due to a gradual decline in prosperity, is shown by the records to have been sudden, to have occurred in January 1577, without record of any public calamity or untoward private expense, or the sale or mortgage of any portion of his land.

". . . the summer of 1577 saw Whitgift . . . conferring with Lucy over the 'discipline' of 'that part of Warwickshire which is in my diocese.' An order had been sent to each bishop to report not only the names of recusants but 'the value of their land and goods, as he shall think they are, not as they are given in the Subsidy Book' and consequently recusants began hiding or handing over to other keeping their goods and valuables, and devising their land to tenants, friends or relatives of less suspicion or wealth.

"John Shakespeare indeed undertook between 1578 and 1580 three otherwise mysterious transactions. On November 12, 1578, he and his wife leased in perpetuity eighty-six acres of land in Wilmcote to Thomas Webbe and Humphrey Hooper . . . on condition that George Gibbes, a friend and neighbour of the Ardens, was to be tenant from September 29, 1580, for twenty-one years on payment to Webbe and Hooper of one quarter of wheat and one quarter of barley annually! Two days after this rather unrewarding conveyance, the Shakespeares mortgaged their house

on Catholics became far stricter owing to the Bull of Excommunication. Before that Catholics had comparatively little to worry about.

Simpson's arguments had a high degree of probability; but they were not a hundred per cent convincing: it was still possible to say there might be other reasons for John Shakespeare's money troubles. The matter was finally settled, however, by Fr Thurston's discoveries concerning the document known as "The Spiritual Testament of John Shakespeare." This parchment was found at the end of the eighteenth century by workmen who were repairing the house of John Shakespeare's descendants, the Harts—the house in Henley Street where William Shakespeare is presumed to have been born and where his parents lived and died. The document, beginning "I, John Shakespeare" and written in a fine Italian hand, was a long and extremely devotional act of Catholic resignation, a sort of guarantee for a happy death, like the devotion of the nine Fridays. Malone, the great eighteenth-century Shakespearian, pronounced it genuine and accepted it enthusiastically, though he was puzzled by the high educational level of the handwriting. But no one else supported him and the document lay neglected for a hundred years. The truth was that Victorian Protestant England simply could not swallow it; the hand-writing and the highly coloured phraseology seemed distressingly foreign, and quite remote from the current notion of an honest Elizabethan burgess. Once again, a complete ignorance of recusant history proved a serious drawback to Shakespearean scholarship. But Fr Thurston's discovery revolutionised the situation, and put the document exactly in its place. In brief, he discovered that it was a formula of prayer devised by St Charles Borromeo, which had enjoyed great popularity towards the end of the sixteenth century. St Charles took a

at Wilmcote, with about fifty acres of land, to their brother-in-law, Edmund Lambert of Barton-on-Heath; and on October 15, 1579, they sold to their nephew, Robert Webbe, their share in the Snitterfield property inherited from Robert Arden. The price of this last was £40, and the final concord was made in April 1580, in which month Alderman John Shakespeare of Stratford had to give securities for his appearance at the Queen's Bench in Westminster in June." *The Slave of Life*, by M. D. H. Parker (Chatto and Windus, 1955) pp. 237–8.

great interest in England; and the English missionary priests who began to come from Rome in 1580 used always to stay with him at Milan on their way. There was a great hunger among English Catholics for devotional works from overseas that kept them in touch with their Faith; so that nothing is more likely than that the missionary priests from Rome, Campion, Persons, Sherwin and their successors, would have brought copies of this popular formula, transcribed into English with a space left blank for the name of the recipient. In fact there *is* a letter from Persons in England to Allen in 1580 asking for hundreds more of "the testaments" because there was such a demand for them. The "testaments" can't refer to the Rheims New Testament which was not yet completed and, in any case would hardly be transportable in hundreds. The obvious reference is to copies of the Spiritual testament, one of which, John Shakespeare's, has survived, a single voice, like a ghost, from the heroic past of our Elizabethan martyrs and confessors.

It was unfortunate that Sir E. K. Chambers in his great biography of Shakespeare, published in 1930, should have quite neglected Thurston's discovery. Sir Edmund accepts John Shakespeare's testament as genuine, but adds: "it probably dates from his early life, and carries little evidence as to his religious position under Elizabeth." But exactly the contrary is the truth. If it dates from any time, it dates from a late period in John Shakespeare's life, from after the coming of the missionary priests. The most likely date is 1580, when Fr Persons who was distributing these leaflets passed through Warwickshire, as he tells us, and was entertained by the Ardens of Parkhall, and also probably by their cousins the Throckmortons of Coughton, only a few miles from Stratford. At that date William Shakespeare would have been sixteen years old. It is an intriguing thought—a meeting between William Shakespeare and Robert Persons. But whether or no that was the actual date, there can be no doubt that during the worst period of persecution Shakespeare's father was a devoutly practising Catholic; and therefore it is more than probable that his earlier financial troubles were for recusancy also—which is equivalent to saying that, as far as we know,

14

during William Shakespeare's childhood and youth, his father was a practising Catholic. The same may be obviously presumed of his mother, all the more so as she was an Arden, second cousin of Edward Arden of Parkhall, High Sheriff of Warwickshire, who was the great prop of Catholicism in the district, from which he took his ancient name, the Forest of Arden, where John Shakespeare also owned land at Wilmcote inherited from his father-in-law, Robert Arden. And at this juncture, let us stress in parenthesis, what nearly everyone is agreed on, that William Shakespeare was brought up much more in the countryside than in the town of Stratford.

We can take it as certain, then, that as long as Shakespeare's parents had any influence over him they brought him up a devoutly practising Catholic. But where could they have practised? Where could Shakespeare have heard Mass? Some, including Professor Dover Wilson, have speculated that in order to have preserved his faith, he would have been sent to the household of his great kinsman, Edward Arden, who was High Sheriff of the county in 1575. But attractive though this speculation is, I would like something more circumstantial; and I think I have it. During Shakespeare's boyhood there was a Mass-centre only six miles from Wilmcote where the Shakespeare's had their little estate: and six miles was no distance for Catholics to travel for the occasional privilege of Mass. This was Coughton, the house of Sir John Throckmorton, Edward Arden's brother-in-law. Now in the Stonyhurst Archives there is a manuscript called "The Life of Edward Throckmorton." Edward Throckmorton, youngest son of the house, was about the same age as Shakespeare, two years older, and since he was a nephew of the Ardens there was also a family connection. We learn from this manuscript that there was great Catholic activity going on around Coughton between 1570 and 1580, that is, between Shakespeare's sixth and sixteenth year. The inspiration of this activity, as in so many other parts of England, was a Catholic schoolmaster, and its chief propagator was young Edward Throckmorton. He was an extremely holy and attractive youth, and quite free from snobbishness, (a vice, says the author of the Life sententiously, "to which young men in this England of ours are regrettably prone.") He left the country in 1580 to be a priest; but before that time it seems unlikely that the Shakespeares living so near, would have escaped his infectious zeal. Under his inspiration, his fellow-pupils, who came from far and wide, organised themselves into a sort of pious death's-head battalion, pledged to martyrdom; they canvassed all the tenants and neighbours round about, especially the poor, to get their boys to the school, and sometimes when they found a boy who was being terrorised from attending, they would smuggle him out at night and hide him in a safe place. They performed various other exploits of holy lawlessness; and in general were a menace to the neighbouring Protestant magistrates, chief of whom was Sir Thomas Lucy. This links up with the tradition of Shakespeare's persecution by the same Sir Thomas Lucy.

Further than this we may not speculate. But while on the subject of Catholic schoolmasters, there is another fact, discovered by Fr Pollen, which is of interest. At the Stratford school which Shakespeare may have attended, there was between the years 1571 and 1575, first as assistant and, then as headmaster, one Simon Hunt who was an active Catholic, probably from his Oxford days; a year or so later he went abroad to the college at Rheims, and in 1578 he became a Jesuit at Rome at the same time as Robert Southwell. It was probably Simon Hunt who supplied some of the materials for the early life of Edward Throckmorton which was written in Rome, though the actual authorship is usually attributed to Robert Southwell. And here I can't omit a slight coincidence which is rather amusing though off the point. In 1586 when it was a question of which Jesuit should go to England, Southwell was eventually chosen, and poor Fr Simon was turned down "for lack of learning"—which may be the explanation of Shakespeare's alleged "little learning and less Greek.": though perhaps I ought to add, that Mr de Wulf noted in the book I mentioned, that the only shcoolmasters Shakespeare is at all scornful about in his plays are obviously Protestant ones; while in *The Taming of the Shrew* he has a sly but friendly reference to a schoolmaster in disguise "that have long been studying at Rheims, so cunning in Greek,

Latin, and other languages." That reference to Rheims is very interesting; Rheims had only one significance for Elizabethans and the friendly tone of Shakespeare's reference is strangely different from that of other contemporary writers.

But to return to certainties. The certainty is that the atmosphere in which Shakespeare was brought up was a sharply recusant one, quite as sharply recusant as that in which another poet, John Donne, was brought up ten years later. And the obvious question I have been leading up to is this: what was its psychological effect on William Shakepeare after he had passed out of his parents influence? We know what its effect on Donne was. Its effect was to make him ask himself: "Do I really believe in this religion for which I am suffering all these drawbacks and dangers?" and to answer, about the age of twenty: "No". He apostatised: and in order to gain political advancement he lent his pen to defame and ridicule the martyrs and confessors of his very own family. We must not judge Donne too harshly; the difficulties and temptations were very great. But we are entitled to state that the temptation to join the more influential Protestant party was equally great for Shakespeare: perhaps greater, because the Earl of Leicester, the Protestant champion, who was the most powerful patron in England, was also particularly influential in Warwickshire.

Are there any signs that Shakespeare like Donne bartered his faith for patronage? The answer is definitely "No." For the period between his marriage and his establishment in London, we have of course very little positive evidence but the indications, such as they are, are in favour of his Catholic loyalty. About this period, romantically called "Shakespeare's Hidden Years" there are only two bits of evidence which are accepted by serious scholars. The first is that supplied by a certain William Beeston, a Catholic actor-manager in the reign of Charles I, who derived it no doubt from his father, Christopher Beeston, who was also an actor-manager and probably also a Catholic. Christopher Beeston was a member of Shakespeare's company for some time, and as other evidence shows, on fairly intimate terms with him. The Beeston evidence which is now generally accepted, is that

"Shakespeare understood Latin pretty well, for he had been in his younger years a schoolmaster in the country. Now Shakespeare had no university degree so that what the evidence probably means is that he was a private tutor at the house of some country gentleman. Under the circumstances, this has a very Catholic ring about it, for the only country gentleman with whom he had family connections were Catholics and recusants. These were the Ardens of Parkhall and their kindred who were wide-spread in various counties. To draw any further inference from Beeston's evidence would again be speculation. But it is interesting that the name of Edward Arden crops up again when we consider the only other bit of evidence about these years, and that is the early tradition already mentioned that Shakespeare was driven out of Warwickshire by the persecution of Sir Thomas Lucy.

The countryside in which Shakespeare lived was terribly divided between Protestants and Catholics. At the head of the Catholic gentry was Edward Arden, who had been High Sheriff of the county, while most prominent among the Protestants, a dependant of the Earl of Leicester and a very determined persecutor, was the magistrate Sir Thomas Lucy, High Sheriff in 1579. Lucy was on all the Commissions which summoned the Catholics, John Shakespeare among them, for recusancy. However as long as Arden retained his local influence, the Catholics were comparatively safe. But the blow came at the end of 1583 when Arden was implicated in one of the most disgustingly bogus plots of the period, nothing but a shameless attempt by Leicester to extirpate his family. Lucy sat on the Commission which indicted him for High Treason: but the actual trial was shifted to London, probably on account of his popularity. He was executed at Tyburn, a martyr in everything but the title. That brings us to 1584, very near the time when Shakespeare fled from Warwickshire. It may also explain how, when he first appears in London, it is with pro-Catholic patrons: Lord Strange and then the young Earl of Southampton. Some details about his feud with Lucy—the deer park and the whippings—have been discredited and are certainly inaccurate, but there is no reason to doubt the essentials of the story and since religion

18

played such a big part in disputes, especially in that district, one is bound to accept the probability that Shakespeare's Catholicism had something to do with his escape to London. It may also explain the matrimonial detail which is usually given a mildly scandalous interpretation. I mean the fact that he got his marriage licence only six months before the birth of his first child. There may have been an earlier Catholic ceremony which was afterwards called in question by the authorities.[1] This of course is only speculation but what one can say is that the indications are in favour of his Catholic loyalty so that we are not surprised to find when, in *As You Like It*, he transforms the Ardenne into the Forest of Arden of his youth, that all his sympathies and a good deal of Catholic imagery are in favour of the exiles and outlaws, while the obviously Protestant vicar, Sir Oliver Martext, is made a fool of, in contrast with the always reverent and often affectionate treatment of Catholic priests and Friars, and Abbesses, and so on, in the earlier plays. Martext's right to perform a marriage ceremony is derided, whereas the validity of Catholic marriage is quite heavily stressed in the contemporary play *Twelfth Night* where sanctity of marriage is insisted on. All this internal evidence I must take for granted because I think it is generally well known and admitted, and content myself with a brief quotation from a Victorian Protestant author:

"To judge from Sir Oliver Martext and Sir Hugh Evans, the parish priests of Shakespeare's day were no very shining lights, and the poet seems to fall back as in *Romeo and Juliet* and *Two Gentlemen of Verona* on the ideal priest of an earlier age. It is indeed true that he always mentions the Old Faith with a certain yearning fondness.

But now that we are beginning to take evidence from the plays themselves great caution is needed. I must remember how deceptive internal evidence is; it can mean just what anyone wants it to mean. It is obviously wrong, for instance, to look for a philosophical message in passages that are sheer

[1] Probably as Miss Parker suggests at Temple Grafton where there was a Marian priest, John Firth, "who had escaped deprivation owing to age, harmlessness and the well-known shortage of new men" and like "Friar Lawrence, in *Romeo and Juliet*, interested in the art of healing, being able to cure sick birds." Ibid., p. 244.

poetry and nothing else, just as it is wrong to wrest the speeches of Shakespeare's characters and claim they are his own opinions. One must respect his creative genius and remember that his job was to be a playwright not a preacher.

All the same in the early plays which I am now considering, it is possible to isolate certain passages or aspects which are Shakespearean yet do not spring from the play itself; they cannot be attributed to its source, its plot, its characters, its tone-value or to dramatic outline, or to stage requirements. These innovations may be as slight as the remark about Rheims I just quoted or as weighty as that decision to refashion the play about *King John* or the Ghost's description of Purgatory in *Hamlet*. But when we meet them we are entitled to say: here is an instance, though maybe a brief and baffling one, of the mind of Shakespeare *outside his play*. These are the only occasions on which we may look for personal opinions that could conceivably, though exaggeratedly, be called "propaganda."

On the subject of propaganda in Elizabethan plays, I must make a short digression. It is sometimes said that the Puritans or extreme Protestants regarded all stage people as atheists and therefore probably Papists as well. But this is misleading. On the contrary, at the beginning of Elizabeth's reign, there was a close alliance between the stage and the Geneva Protestants for propaganda purposes. The alliance did not succeed but it survived. In 1583 the first official companies of players were formed by extreme Protestants—Leicester and Walsingham. When Shakespeare first came to London it was quite common for an actor or playwright to be a government spy, and some of the most prominent authors—Munday, Greene, Peel, knew how to be bitterly anti-Catholic.

So that if Shakespeare really was a pro-Catholic playwright, then he was ploughing a lonely furrow when he began.

For the sake of making the gap in his life as short as possible, I will take what was probably his first play *The Comedy of Errors*: it can be dated with good reason to the winter of 1588-9.

I hesitated at first about bringing forward this evidence, but have decided to so so, because it is not mine: it was objectively arrived at by an American scholar, Professor Baldwin, who, I believe enjoys a high reputation. He has no interest in Catholicism. All he wants to do is to show that in the first and last scenes of the comedy Shakespeare was influenced by an actual execution which took place in October 1588, in front of Burbage's theatre in Holywell, Shoreditch, where Shakespeare then was. The *Comedy* is mainly a Wodehousian farce, but the first and last scenes stand quite apart, and are quite serious. In the first scene a "reverend Syracusan merchant" is being sentenced to death, not for any crime against the natural law, but for breaking the Statute which forbade Syracusan merchants to set foot in Ephesus. The Duke of Ephesus says he is sorry for the "reverend merchant" who is personally guiltless, but the law is a just reprisal against the Syracusans, and must take its course. In the last scene the "reverend merchant" is being led to the place of execution which is beside an abbey or convent of nuns, and is described as—

> " . . . the melancholy vale,
> The place of death and sorry execution
> Beside the ditches of the abbey here." (v. i. 120-2)

At the critical juncture the Abbess comes out of her convent and pleads in a way that makes the Duke change his mind, and all ends happily.

But what struck Baldwin was that opposite Shakespeare's theatre there was the ditch or conduit that ran from Shoreditch to the City, and there was Holywell Priory, the famous old convent of nuns dissolved in 1539. And it was at Holywell, opposite the theatre—as Stowe's *Chronicles* expressly notes— that Blessed William Hartley and others were butchered in October 1588.

In the wave of blood-lust that was let loose after the Armada, thirty priests were executed in different places of London, chosen as object lessons to Catholic sympathisers who might be living there. According to Baldwin, Shakespeare transmogrified in his play the fleeting impression of a scene he had actually witnessed, and he used the term "merchant" which was how the priests always described themselves in their letters. His theory may sound a bit thin in my

21

crude summary; but I must say after reading his full exposition I was as convinced as one can be by that type of argument. But when Baldwin turns aside to discuss how his theory bears on Shakespeare's religious opinions, his conclusion is the inevitably superficial one that Shakespeare was a fair-minded man who liked to see both sides of a question and disliked "intolerance" in any form. But that sort of conclusion will not stand up against the savage background of 1588. If Shakespeare was really hinting in public at a plea for toleration, as Baldwin supposes, then he was going further than any neutral-minded man dared to go at that time, and as far as any Catholic would go who was not bent on martyrdom. Of course you may think that Baldwin's reconstruction is all moonshine. But I have chosen to stand by it, and I think it agrees with a veiled plea for mercy and reconciliation that runs through many of Shakespeare's plays from first to last: you get it exemplified in *King John*: there is a glimpse of it in the *Merchant of Venice*; it is very cogently reasoned in *Measure for Measure*; and finally in one of his last plays *Cymbeline* it is directly related to the spiritual authority of the Court of Rome.

But now for more certain evidence I turn to two plays, *King John* and *Henry IV* and here I would stress once more the distinction between his creative genius and his individual standpoint. From a dramatic point of view the most important thing in the play *King John* is the creation of Falconbridge, and the most important thing in the play *Henry IV* is the creation of the immortal Falstaff. Yet these plays also supply us with clear evidence about Shakespeare's *de facto* attitude to the Catholic Church as a subject of historical controversy in his day. What is more there is evidence that many of his contemporaries judged this attitude of his to be the most important thing about the plays, and found it so offensive as to quite outweigh any question of his creative genius. But here I must digress again to say a few words about Protestant propagandist history in the reign of Queen Elizabeth I.

All history in the century was either mere chronicle or sheer propaganda. All who handled history, for instance, were frankly biased in favour of Lancastrians as against

22

Yorkists: Catholics even more than others, because the Lancastrian kings in spite of their faults were all great and pious benefactors of the Church. England's Catholic past was, of course, a favourite plank of Catholic controversialists, whose books, though prohibited, were fairly widely read. But by Shakespeare's time there was already a Protestant version of England's past which was rapidly gaining ground. Its chief authors in succession were: Bayle, the apostate friar and Protestant bishop, about 1550; John Foxe of Foxe's Martyrs, about 1570; and finally Shakespeare's contemporary, John Speed, who was a very considerable historian in his own right —though he is little quoted nowadays. There were three crucial points on which these propagandists sought to change the traditional story handed down by "monkish chroniclers" or by popular sentiment. The first was Papal aggression in the reign of King John; Bayle and Foxe presented John as a hero and as the great patriotic precursor of Henry VIII. The second point concerned the Lollards as "the morning stars" of the Reformation, with particular emphasis on Sir John Oldcastle: Foxe presented him as a noble figure which in a way he was, and as the first Protestant martyr, though in fact, as Robert Persons pointed out to the great annoyance of John Speed, Oldcastle died a Catholic. The third point was the Royal Divorce and here they had to counteract sentiments that were almost within the living memory of Londoners, namely the reverence felt of Katherine of Aragon as a heroine, and for Sir Thomas More as a hero. Shakespeare handled all these questions, notably that for Katherine of Aragon and Saint Thomas More: but since there is doubt and dispute about his share in these plays, I will omit them here and deal only with the other two.

Bayle's vitriolic play about King John had been modernised by an unknown Protestant dramatist in 1591. In this play, called *The Troublesome Reign of King John*, John is a clear-cut hero with resounding echoes of England's recent stand against Pope and Armada; the Papal Legate, Pandulph, is an utterly slimey and crawling twister; and there are scenes of lechery between monks and nuns. Shakespeare handled the same theme a year or so later. It is enough to say that, under his treatment, John appears as an unbalanced tyrant declining into frenzy; the Papal Legate Pandulph is a dignified figure, with arguments very like Fr Persons's, not warmly attractive it is true, but always reasonable, always in command of the situation, and finally rescuing England from invasion by his moderate and sensible counsels. The scenes about monks and nuns are entirely eliminated. Comparatively speaking it is an amazing transformation—and, incidentally, it quite ruins the dramatic unity of the older play. Commentators attempting to explain it have suggested that he wrote it to please his Catholic or pro-Catholic patrons. But that only throws us back on the fact that his having such patrons shows his own pro-Catholic leanings. The obvious conclusion is that Shakespeare intended the natural consequences of his act, which were to restore the traditional Catholic view as against the Protestant version which the recent defeat of the Armada would have made much more popular and plausible, Shakespeare was consciously swimming against the tide.

In dealing with the myth of King John as the first Protestant Patriot Shakespeare used reason and rhetoric. But when he came to the myth of Oldcastle as the first Protestant martyr, he employed the much more devastating weapon of laughter; he blew it away in a great gale of good humour. It is quite certain that in the first part of *Henry IV* as composed by Shakespeare and as first played on the stage, the immortal character we know as Falstaff was called Sir John Oldcastle; the name Falstaff was added later to avoid trouble. The Oldcastle of history was in fact the friend and adviser of Henry V in his youth, but after the coronation renounced his loyalty rather than give up his opinions. The only evidence that he encouraged the Prince in riotous living comes, paradoxically, from Foxe himself who says that Oldcastle was guided by interior light to abandon his early vices. But that—plus the fact that some indecent writings, which he disowned, were found in his house—was quite enough to start the unjust picture of the typical Puritan who glosses his carnal vices with a pious text from Scripture. Shakespeare chose to present his Oldcastle as a hoary old hypocrite who quotes the Geneva Bible almost every second line; but then he enters into the fun of the thing and makes him parody his own hypocrisy, and fills him with an irresistible zest for life until he becomes the glorious unregenerate whom Englishmen are so fond of in fancy—and so stern against in fact. Queen Elizabeth, we are told, laughed as heartily as anybody. But there were politicians close to the Government who did not find this travesty of Foxe's first martyr at all funny. In the next year a smug and vindictive Protestant play inspired by Lord Cobham, Cecil's brother-in-law appeared. Written mainly by the Government spy, Anthony Munday, it presented Old-castle as the saintly victim of immoral priests and monks. But it was quite futile. The damage was done. There would be no Martyrs Memorial to Oldcastle. Shakespeare changed the name fortunately for posterity; so that we can enjoy Falstaff without the shadow of controversy. But the resentment lingered for half a century after his death; and during his lifetime it was expressed with some bitterness by John Speed.

Speed was engaged in trying to rescue Bayle's and Foxe's version of history from the attacks of Robert Persons, when he found his picture of Oldcastle blown to pieces by rude laughter. In an extraordinary passage of his History he couples *Robert Persons* and *William Shakespeare* as fellow-conspirators in a campaign of lying propaganda. Having accused Persons—quite untruthfully as it happens—of making Oldcastle "a Ruffian, a Robber, and a Rebel," he adds:

> And his (Persons's) authority, taken from the stage-players, is more befitting the pen of his slanderous report than the credit of the judicious, being only grounded from this Papist and his poet, of like conscience for lies, the one ever feigning and the other ever falsifying the truth ...

"This Papist and his Poet"—i.e. Persons and Shakespeare— "the one ever feigning, and the other ever falsifyng the truth." Speed is evidently harking back to other sore points—like the play about King John—and harking forward also (for this book was not published till 1611) to later plays by Shakespeare. What he suggests is, of course fantastic; that there was actual collaboration between Persons and Shakespeare. But Speed was not a fanatic; he was intelligent and aimed at being judicious. There must have been some ground for his accusation; and the only possible ground is that Shakespeare's plays in his lifetime were believed to be guardedly but consistently pro-Catholic. I would say that Speed's accusation clinches the other evidence I have given, and establishes a strong presumption of Shakespeare's loyalty to his recusant upbringing—so strong that anyone who questions it should be asked to produce positive evidence for doing so.

My case really rests there, with Speed. But I can't leave untouched a much more vital question. So far I have only shown Shakespeare's outlook in his earlier plays, and in accidental issues, minor points of controversy and custom. But was he *Essentially* Catholic, especially in his later and greater plays where he moved more freely and profoundly among the issues of life and death that are bound up with religion? The difficulty here is one of interpretation. Once we begin to talk about Shakespeare's "message to humanity" and so on, we come against a thousand cogent and passionate theories as to what it was, varying from profound pessimism to triumphant optimism: from stoic fatalism to Christian resignation. For example: I could provide an interpretation of *Hamlet* as a great Catholic tragedy—the tragedy of lost faith—beginning with the soul from Purgatory, the Ghost of the old religion, and ending with the echo from the proscribed Catholic burial service; and "flights of Angels sing thee to thy rest." "*In Paradisum deducant te Angeli.*" But at the end all you could say would be: "Very nice, very interesting, but is it Shakespeare?" So we must sadly abandon plays like *Hamlet* and *Lear* which admit of two interpretations. Fortunately, however, we have one great play which, though often misunderstood, admits of only one main interpretation, that which Shakespeare worked out clearly as stated in its title: *Measure for Measure*. And here I follow in the essentials (where they agree) three English scholars—R. W. Chambers, Wilson Knight, and F. R. Leavis—who have made sense of the play in a manner that does not allow contradiction. The theme, stated in the title, is the teaching of Our Lord:

Judge not and ye shall not be judged. For with what judgement you judge you shall be judged: and with what measure you mete, it shall be measured to you again. (Matt. vii, 2.)

with the accompanying verses that teach forgiveness of
26

enemies, and condemn hypocrisy. The play traces with extreme care and subtlety the working out of heavenly justice in the actual and sordid circumstances of justice on this earth; besides being an exciting story, it is strictly didactic and allegorical. The Duke is the agent of heavenly justice: Angelo, the Deputy is the majesty of positive law which is corrupt within; Isabella is fiery chastity that has not yet reached perfect true charity, and so on. The play is worked out beautifully to the last detail. Just one example: when Mariana pleads for her lover, she is earthly love doing what even the pagans do; but when Isabella finally pleads, she is Christian charity "praying for them that persecute you"; and the result, though she does not expect it, is that her brother whom she thought dead is restored to life. Measure for measure— "pressed down, and shaken together and running over shall they give into your bosom"[1] for she also wins the Duke; but the marriage is only hinted at, not stated so as to give it not a sensual, but an allegorical and even mystical meaning. In short it is the only great religious play that has graced the English stage between the Middle Ages and T. S. Eliot. That it *is* a great Christian play all sensible commentators are agreed. But my point is that it is a great Christian play worked out in terms of explicitly *Roman* Catholic, Papist symbols: the proscribed habits of St Francis and St Clare, and the proscribed Sacrament of Confession and Absolution. There were also for those who cared to hear them, many echoes of approval for Catholic casuistry and of reproach for the penal laws and their hypocritical administrators. Of course all that would have to be worked out against the background of popular feeling at the time (1602) and of the number of Catholics who attended plays, and so on; and I must admit my three authorities would not agree with me on these last points. Also, of course, it's always possible to argue that what Shakespeare taught in his plays is no evidence of his private belief. Still this play must be chalked up as heavily in favour of his Catholicism. If he believed in any one religion, he believed in the Catholic Church. But perhaps those most inclined to deny *Measure for Measure* to be a Catholic play, would be

[1] Luke vi. 38.

27

Catholics themselves. The seamy side—it might be argued—bulks far too large. Here—as in other of the later plays—there is a plethora of words like "rank" and "stench" and "stews" and "ooze," which seem to cloud the very atmosphere through which one sees or reads the play. But here it is necessary that our judgement of Shakespeare should be not absolute but comparative. Take a course of reading in the other Jacobean dramatists—Chapman, Fletcher, Marston, Tourneur, even Jonson who was by way of being a Catholic: the dominant impression you get is of evil acquiesced in, of innocence lost and no attempt being made to recover it. The truth is that the times were very evil; and the strength of these other dramatists lies in the presentation of evil; their good characters with the exception of Webster's superb Duchess of Malfi—are feeble and conventional. To read them for long is to get the effect of a London fog, opaque and often greasy between earth and heaven. Shakespeare too was confronted by this murky wall; but he did not acquiesce in it. He fought against it. When he is gross and violent it is often for that reason, that he is fighting his way through. He did not take refuge in merely sentimental idealism. He took the tangle of human nature as he found it—fiendishly wicked as it was in high places, and bestially ignorant in low—and he found a way to let in the light of heavenly grace. The imagery of grace is markedly present in the last plays.

I have spoken of the difficulty of interpretation, of attempting to assess Shakespeare's views of life from his plays. Yet I think most people are agreed that what makes the last plays peculiarly attractive is that they are the reflection of a great man who plunged deep into despair, yet refused to give up hope. As he said in *The Tempest*, in his last epilogue:

> And my ending is despair
> Unless I be relieved by prayer
> Which pierces so that it assaults
> Mercy itself, and frees all faults.

It is always a dubious process to try and work stage-effects back into the real life of their author. But I think it ought to be said that there is no reason for *not* holding that Shakespeare was a very *good* man as well as a very great man.

We have only one grain of real evidence about his private life, but it is a grain worth more than tons of speculation. It comes—perhaps significantly—from the Catholic actor Christopher Beeston, who knew him in 1598 and perhaps shared rooms with him.

"He lived in Shoreditch," says Beeston meditatively, "and was the more to be admired because he was *not* a company-keeper, and would not be debauched." And he adds the quaint detail: "When invited to writ, he was in pain."

No wonder he was in pain when he wrote. Like all great poets he was in a sense a mediator between nature and grace. *But* he had no great Catholic philosophy to help him to reconcile grace and nature; no mighty synthesis of Aquinas or Scotus like Dante had to sustain him. All *that* had gone with the Middle Ages. In persecuted England, the Catholic emphasis was all—it had to be—on discipline and devotion and moral theology. Shakespeare, like the *jongleur* before the statue of Our Lady, had to fall back on his own trade. He had to work out the reconciliation of nature and grace in the terms of the things he knew how to handle: fables and allegories and stage-devices—like the trick at the end of *The Winter's Tale* when the Italian statue smiles and comes to life—which incidentally has a very popish and baroque atmosphere about it.

But here I must break off, for it is not my job to interpret the great plays. I would only say that we have no reason to be surprised when we come to the last bit of external evidence. It is supplied by the worthy Archdeacon Davies who concluded his notes on Shakespeare with the famous last words: "HE DYED A PAPIST."[1] It is evidence that has been indignantly rejected. But it is good evidence; and we have the cautious but firm and fair conclusion of Sir E. K. Chambers that there is no valid reason for rejecting it.

But if there is no valid reason for rejecting it, I think the other evidence I have collected gives us a valid reason for accepting it. Indeed I think the evidence I have presented goes further than that. It enables us to maintain, not only that he died a papist, but that he lived a papist also.

[1] Richard Davies, Vicar of Sapperton, and later Archdeacon of Coventry. (MS. Oxf. 31577.)

Hamlet's Divinity

HAMLET is littered with scraps of Divinity. It might be worth seeing what happens when they are put together. The first batch centres on the Ghost. The second concerns Hamlet's spiritual struggles. There is also a third batch. A *prima facie* case exists for a theological theme in the first batch; Hamlet's veering opinions on the Ghost—a soul from Purgatory or a fiend from Hell—hinged on a very topical point of controversy. By Article 23, and the Act of Uniformity, all ghosts must necessarily be devils; to Catholics on the other hand, they would be welcome ocular proof of the traditional doctrine.[1] Shakespeare's introduction of *Wittenberg* might be a device for linking Hamlet's hesitation sympathetically with the religious waverings of his audience.

> If there be any good thing to be done
> Which may to thee do ease and grace to me:
> (I. i. 130–1)

Horatio's words present the doctrine of the merit and efficacy

---

[1] In "What Happens in *Hamlet*" Professor Dover Wilson leaves us, at the end of Act 1, with the sceptic, the Catholic, and the Protestant—representing a typical audience of the time—each eager for the confirmation of a different hypothesis: that the Ghost is an illusion or a soul from Purgatory—or a fiend from Hell. In fact these are precisely the three hypotheses that Horatio runs through in his first coherent address to the Ghost. First he speaks to the disciple of Reginald Scot:
> Stay, illusion!
> If thou hast any sound, or use of voice,
> Speak to me. (I. i. 127–9)
Then, as a Catholic and finally as a Protestant assuming a body more probably for evil purposes, one of those maleficent creatures who burrowed underground like "pioners or diggers for metal."
> If thou art privy to thy country's fate,
> Which happily foreknowing may avoid,
> O, speak!
> Or if thou hast uphoarded in thy life
> Extorted treasure in the womb of the earth,
> For which, they say, you spirits oft walk in death,
> Speak of it: stay, and speak! (I. i. 133–8)

30

of prayers for the dead, strenuously denied by Bishop Jewell, the Anglican spokesman, and as strenuously affirmed by Dr Allen for the Catholics. The controversy continued till the end of the century; its high literary level was noted by Gabriel Harvey and Edmund Bolton. The present context, however, is not controversial. Horatio goes on with two more "if" clauses which might be classed as "popular superstitions." Prayers for the dead lingered nostalgically in England long after their official prohibition. A nostalgic evocation of childhood beliefs characterises the other scraps of Divinity in this scene.[1]

On the first departure of the Ghost, Horatio comments:

> The cock, that is the trumpet to the morn,
> Doth with his lofty and shrill-sounding throat
> Awake the god of day: and, at his warning,
> Whether in sea or fire, in earth or air,
> The extravagant and erring spirit hies
> To his confine. (I. i. 148–56)

These lines are a lovely paraphrase of those in the Liturgy for Sunday Lauds, from the cock-crow hymn of St Ambrose:

> Praeco diei iam sonat,
> Jubarque solis evocat,
> Hos excitatus lucifer
> Solvit polum caligine:
> Hoc omnis erronum cohors
> Viam nocendi deserit.[2]

Marcellus's rejoinder, in the lines that follow, recalls the other cock-crow hymn of the Liturgy, the *Ales diei nuntius* of Prudentius, for Tuesday Lauds; but Marcellus throws in some additional folk-lore about Christmas which makes Horatio say, "So have I heard, and do *in part* believe it." (I. i. 165)

Encouraged by one fairly obvious reference to the Roman Breviary, one may find another in Hamlet's first reaction to

---

[1] *Hamlet* quotations are from Dowden's edition: *The Arden Shakespeare*, 1909.
[2] "The herald of the morning sounds, and calls out the sun-ray. Wakened by him the day-star frees the sky from darkness: at his note the troops of prowling outlaws forsake their baleful course." "Extravagant and erring" looks like an etymological rendering of the Latin words *erro, erronis*, meaning "a lawless vagabond."

31

the Ghost, "Angels and ministers of grace defend us"
(I. iv. 39.) For the prayer in the Office of St Michael, "May
we be defended on earth by thy ministers in heaven" is
accompanied by an antiphon which invokes the Angelic protection *HIC ET UBIQUE* (I. v. 136.) An ironic echoing of
the Liturgy may be sufficient explanation of Hamlet's odd
irruption into Latinity, "Hic et ubique!", when the Ghost
moans beneath him.

In contrast with these friendly scraps of the Liturgy, the
Ghost's credentials are presented with harsh and dogmatic
realism. Here is no classic shade or casual echo of popular
superstition.

> I am thy father's spirit:
> Doom'd for a certain term to walk the night,
> And for the day confined to fast in fires,
> Till the foul crimes done in my days of nature
> Are burnt and purged away. But that I am forbid
> To tell the secrets of my prison-house,
> I could a tale unfold whose lightest word
> Would harrow up thy soul, freeze thy young blood . . .
>   (I. v. 9–16)

The atmosphere is the strongly *pre-Tridentine* one that clung
to Elizabethan Catholicism. Their books of devotion depicted
the pains of Purgatory as equal to those of Hell in actual
severity, different only in duration; Hell was eternal, Purgatory temporal. From Hell there was no return, but souls from
Purgatory could revisit earth to issue warnings or solicit
prayers. Dr A. C. Southern quotes examples to show that
some such phrases as "whence there is no return" was, for
Elizabethan Catholics, the distinguishing mark between Hell
(meaning Purgatory) and Hell proper.[1]

The Council of Trent in its last session, 1563, had firmly
disengaged the essential doctrine of Purgatory from sensational apparitions; and in a popular work such as Persons's
Christian Directory, written in 1582 the milder and more
rational view is apparent. But Dr Allen in 1565, in his
Declaration and Defence of Purgatory, could still write,

[1] Southern, *Elizabethan Recusant Prose 1559–1582* (Sands, 1950), p.
225. The author suggests this phrase as a solution of the *crux* in *Hamlet*,
III. i. 80.

"Sometimes also by the force of the same spirit, the departed have appeared among the living . . .," and could comment

> Marry as these must be the most secret ways and unknown steps of God's Spirit, and therefore most humbly reverenced of the faithful, so because they are so far from the raze of natural affairs, and much over-reach flesh and blood, they are often of fools contemned, and of the unwise wisdom of worldlings as extreme madness improved.[1]

This is the sort of background that corresponds to Hamlet's reactions to the Ghost:

> . . . And we fools of nature
> So horridly to shake our dispositions
> With thoughts beyond the reaches of our souls?
>
>   (I. iv. 53–5)

and:

> There are more things in heaven and earth, Horatio
> Than are dreamt of in your philosophy. (I. v. 166–7)

It was a background shared, or debated, by not a few patrons of the theatre. About 1595, in certain Catholic circles connected with the Court, there was a story current of the ghost of Lord Stourton appearing in flames and soliciting prayers.[2]

The word "prison-house" used by the Ghost, recalls a whole chapter of the controversy between Jewell and Allen. It may be worth mentioning because it centred round a text which seems to have been in Shakespeare's mind in Hamlet's death-scene.

> Be at agreement speedily with thy adversary whilst thou art with him in the way; lest that adversary deliver thee to the judge, and thy judge deliver thee to the sergeant, by whom thou may be cast into prison. Surely I say unto thee, thou shall not get out till thou hast discharged the uttermost farthing. (Matt. v, 24–6)

Though this is not the exact text of the Genevan version—

[1] Allen, *A Defense of Purgatory* (Antwerp, 1565), p. IIIv.

[2] It may also be worth noting—in connection with Hamlet's "Yes by Saint Patrick!"—that stories of the harrowing sights seen in St Patrick's Purgatory would be familiar to those who had served against the O'Neils in Ulster. As early as 1571, Edmund Campion, in his *History of Ireland*, gave a long description of the place "because I would be discharged of the expectation of my readers"—though he himself adds a rider to the effect—"that in the drift and strength of Imagination, a contemplative person would happely suppose the sight of many strange things which he never saw." Quoted by Southern in the book already cited, pp. 295–7. This author also, p. 225, suggests a connection between recusant prayer-books and *Hamlet*, III. i. 80.

the one most used by Shakespeare[1]—the use of the word *sergeant*, for the official who arrested for debt, is certainly Genevan.

The "sergeant" in this text was generally interpreted as Death—"dread Sergeant of th'Eternal Judge." The Catholic argument was that imprisonment after death, till a debt was paid, signified the temporal punishment of Purgatory. What makes it likely that Shakespeare had the same text in mind in Act Five is that Hamlet's line about the "fell sergeant, death" occurs in the context of "exchanging forgiveness" with his adversary Laertes—though not of course, with Claudius.

A more obvious instance of a divinity-reference, dropped in the First Act and then picked up again later on, is the Ghost's lament, "Unhousel'd, disappointed, unaneled," (I. v. 76) to which a stage tradition gives young Hamlet the reply, "Oh, horrible! Oh, horrible! most horrible!" (I. v. 80). Catholic horror at death without the sacraments returns in III. iii. 60–4, when Hamlet finds Claudius praying:

> He took my father grossly, full of bread,
> With all his crimes broad blown, as flush as May:
> And how his audit stands who knows save heaven?
> But in our circumstances and course of thought
> 'Tis heavy with him.

Hamlet therefore postpones revenge until he can catch Claudius, as Claudius caught his father, in mortal sin. The views of critics on this scene are: *either* that Hamlet is using theology as a cloak to cover his repugnance, moral or sensitive, at killing a helpless victim, *or*, alternatively, that the scene is a lump of pre-existent melodrama imperfectly digested by Shakespeare. Either view would write *finis* to any religious interest in Hamlet. His profession of belief would be either shamefacedly self-deceptive, or shamelessly out-of-character. My essay would end here, were it not that I cannot bring myself to accept either the one view or the other.

The one clashes too violently with the ensuing scene, in

[1] Cf. Noble: *Shakespeare's Biblical Knowledge* (S.P.C.K. 1935), *passim*. The author does not include this text among his instances.

34

which Hamlet's behaviour is quite brazenly bloodthirsty and puritanical. The other jars too obviously against Hamlet's advice to the players, where Shakespeare expressly warns his actors against melodramatic stage-tricks, and invites the audience to look for a subtler theme than blood-and-thunder —for nothing less than the imprint of their own restless minds on the passage of time. My original suggestion was that the divinity-references in *Hamlet* are meant by Shakespeare to engage, consciously or unconsciously, the religious hesitations of his listeners. I think it can be applied to III. iii, to reconcile what is true in both the preceding theories. But a good deal more evidence will be needed.[1]

The conclusion from the first batch of references was the contrast between the easy natural piety (a mixture of Liturgy and folk-lore) that precedes the Ghost's credentials, and the harsh breath of supernatural realism that comes in with the Ghost's credentials. It is the contrast between the *comfort* of the Old Religion, in wistful retrospect, and its *authority*, risen from the grave, and issuing political directives on a par with its revealed doctrine. At first Hamlet does not feel the contrast; his feelings towards the Ghost may be put in words transposed from another scene:

> His form and cause conjoin'd preaching to stones
> Would make them capable. (III. iv. 125–6)

But it is not long before the Ghost's "form" (the sensible appeal of his ruined glory) and his "cause" (political action

[1] Among Protestants there was a nostalgic longing for the ritual and reverence of the Old Religion, especially for its funeral rites and its reverence for the dead. Typical of this attitude were: Nashe's *Christ's Tears over Jerusalem*, Drayton's *Legend of Cromwell*, Spelman's *History of Sacrilege*: It was an attitude which would shortly find an outlet in the Anglo-Catholic movement. On the other hand among the born Catholics, there was a falling-off from the first impetus of the Counter Reformation: this was especially marked at the turn of the century, when dissensions broke out amongst them, skilfully fomented by Government propagandist—chief among whom was Samuel Harsnet, with his book on the supposed exorcism of spirits. Among individuals of the play-going type, there was a fairly steady two-way traffic, of which Shakespeare was certainly aware—
> Out of these Convertites
> There is much matter to be heard and learned.
> (*As You Like It*, V. iv. 191–2)

here and now) begin to drift apart. His *form* has filled Hamlet with a melting desire for solitude and contemplation: "For mine own poor part, look you, I'll go pray." But already the *cause* has become a source of nagging disquiet:

> The time is out of joint—O cursed spite,
> That ever I was born to set it right. (I. v. 188–9)

This uneasiness will serve as a question-mark to open up the second batch of references, those concerning Hamlet's spiritual struggles. Hamlet's tendency to preach points to the use of some book of divinity. I propose to take Robert Persons's *Christian Directory* as a typical devotional work of the period. Its popularity, both among Protestants and Catholics, was rivalled only by Granada's "Meditations"[1] but Persons uses a bracing, salty prose more reminiscent of *Hamlet* than the Granada translations are. Here are some examples:[2]

> "these bugs and fancies of imagined difficulties", "This is the market wherein we must buy."

Or, for longer extracts:

> Pride is but a point of gentry: gluttony, good fellowship: anger and revenge, but an effect of courage: lechery and wantonesse, a trick of youth: They shall find one day that these excuses will not be received.

> You shall see many men in the world, with whom, if you talk of a cow or a calf, of a fat ox, of a piece of ground, or the like, they can both hear and talk willingly and freshly: But if you reason with them of their salvation, and of their inheritance in the kingdom of heaven, they answer not at all, but will hear as if in a dream.

> And further than this, the evil hath this perogrative above the good in our life: that one defect onely overwhelmeth and drowneth a great number of pleasurers together. As if a man had all the felicities together which this world could yield, and yet had but one tooth out of tune: all the other pleasures would not make him merry.

The first reminiscence of devotional literature comes in Hamlet's speech to Rosencrantz and Guildenstern, explaining

---

[1] Cf. Hagedorn, *Reformation und Spanische Andachtsliteratur* (Leipzig, 1934.)

[2] Quotations are from a 1650 edition, which reproduces the second and enlarged edition of 1585.

his desolation (II. ii) "What a piece of work is man, etc."
The basic reference here is to Psalm Eight. But a typical
working out of the text is exemplified in this passage of
Persons's: In particular, Hamlet's phrase, "How infinite in
faculty! in form and moving, how express and admirable!"
finds its place in the argument:

> In the body of Man, which for his beauty and variety is called *The
> Little World*: the veins, which are without number, have all one begin-
> ning in the liver: the arteries in the heart: the sinews in the brain. And
> that which is more, the infinite actions of life, sense and reason in man:
> as generations, corruptions, nourishments, digestions, and altera-
> tions, feeling, smelling, tasting, seeing, hearing, moving, speaking,
> thinking, remembering, discoursing: and ten hundred thousand parti-
> cular actions, operations and motions besides, which are exercised in
> man's body under these and other such names and appellations: all
> these (I say) being infinite in number most admirable in order, and
> distinct in their every office and operation: do receive not withstanding,
> their beginning from one most simple unity and indivisible substance
> called the Soul, which produceth, governeth, and directeth them all to
> so innumerable, different and contrary functions.
>
> By this concludeth the Metaphysick, that as among the creatures,
> we finde this most excellent order and connection of things, whereby
> one bringeth forth many, and every multitude is referred to his unity:
> so much more, in all reason, must the whole frame of creatures con-
> teined in this world (wherein there are so many millions of multitudes
> with their unities,) be referred to one most simple and abstract unity,
> that gave beginning to them all. And this is God.

This long extract is part of a series of suasions, some of
them based on the Ptolemaic universe, for belief in Divine
Providence. Comparison with Hamlet's speech, similar in
phrasing but wholly dissimilar in intention, shows that he
has lost the easy, natural piety of the First Act. He is saying
in effect: "The beautiful plan of the mediaeval universe has
faded. So I am beginning to doubt the beauty, if not the
existence, of God the Planner." The only antidote to religious
scepticism will henceforth be a dreary puritanical sense of duty.

The second reminiscence makes a link between two passages—Hamlet's list of injustices in the "To be or not to be"
soliloquy and his overwhelming sense of Original Sin as
expressed to Ophelia immediately afterwards. The paragraph in Persons's is entitled "The facility of Sinning," and

the section-heading is, "The world is misery," in the chapter "Against Love of the World."

> Let him walk out into the streets, behold the doings of men, view their behaviour, consider what is said and treated in Shops, in Halls in Consistories, in Judgement-seats, in Palaces, and in common meeting-places abroad. He shall find that of all things whereof men do make any account in the world, nothing is so little accounted of as to commit sinne. He shall see Justice sold, Verity wrested, Shame lost, and Equity disguised. He shall see the innocent condemned, the guilty delivered, the wicked advanced, the virtuous oppressed. He shall see many thieves flourish, many usurers bear great sway, many murderers and extortioners reverenced and honoured, many fools put in authority: and divers which have nothing in them, but the bare shape and form of men, by reason of money to be placed in great dignities for the government of others. He shall hear at every man's mouth almost, vanity, pride, detraction, envy, deceit, dissimulation, wantonesse, dissolution, lying, swearing, perjury, and blasphemie. Finally he shall see the most part of men to govern themselves absolutely, even as beasts do, by the motion of their passions, not by the laws of Justice, Reason, Religion, or Virtue, and hereby he may frame his conceit of the world in this behalf.

Various other passages in *Hamlet* may be recalled here, and also Shakespeare's Sonnet LXVI. The conclusion, from consideration of sin in the world, is the same in the Soliloquy as in the Sonnet: "Tired with all these, for restful death I cry." Persons's conclusion of course was: "shun the world and take up the religious life." Once again we have Hamlet taking a divinity-context and giving it an egocentric twist Perhaps a pattern is beginning to emerge. In the previous reference was saw Beauty withdrawing from Religion, and leaving scepticism as the result, to sap the motives of conscience and honest living. Now in the "To be or not to be" Soliloquy, we see Beauty returning as the Death-wish, and championing heroic action, *in opposition to* conscience which is now in alliance, oddly, with sloth and scruples. Hamlet, as he says to Ophelia, has divorced "the power of beauty" from "the force of honesty." But Beauty and honesty have met again, as enemies, and, like the duellists, have changed rapiers.

Hamlet's easy coupling of "bestial oblivion" with "thinking too precisely on the event," which is on the face of it paradoxical, may be explained by a passage of Persons's on sloth and scruples.

> All these and many more are the effects of sloth: but these four essentially have I thought good to touch in this place, for that they let and hinder greatly this resolution which we talk of. For he that liveth in a slumber, and will not hear or attend to anything that is said of the life to come: and besides this, imagineth fearfull matters in the same: and thirdly is thrown down by every little block that he findeth in the way: and lastly, is so lazy as he can bear no labour at all: this man (I say) is past hope to be gained to any such purpose as we speak of.

In revenge, as it were, for the *mésalliance* of beauty with heroic action in the death-wish, Hamlet's aggressive honesty misappropriates concupiscence, which should be the province of beauty. Instead of the grim calm of a lawful executioner, we see a gloating lust whipped up by such phrases as, "I'll tent him to the quick", "to see the puppets dallying", "Now could I drink hot blood." He even falls back on ambition and envy as secondary motives. Persons has a passage on this sort of confusion of motives:

> Another cause of vexation in these men is, for that these passions of disordinate concupiscence be oftentimes contrary the one to the other, and do demand most opposite and contrary things, representing to us most lively the confusion of *Babel*, where one tongue spoke against another, and that in diverse and contrary languages. So we see oftentimes that the desire of honour saith to his master: *Spend here*; but the passion of avarice saith: *Hold thy hands*. Lechery saith: *Venture here*: but Pride saith *No, it may turn thee to dishonour*. Anger saith: *Revenge thyself here*; but Ambition saith: *It is better to dissemble*.

Yet, all the while, he is aware of how far he has fallen from the complete self-dedication of Act I. "Lapsed in time and passion." "Lapsed" should, I think, be taken as "snared." "Time," in the sense of "The time is out of joint," means politics. "Passion" is the concupiscence he had thought conquered, which has crept back in the guise of duty. The return of the Ghost fills him with overwhelming sadness; it is the last flicker of his Old Religion: "Look you how pale he glares."[1] Having churned out his dreary sermon to his

[1] Hamlet's "bloody thoughts", in IV. iv., are obviously divorced from any spiritual allegiance to the Ghost. The visionary effects of the Ghost's visitation (prayer, fasting, tenderness, etc.) have done nothing but complicate his powers of action. He thrusts them aside, when entangled in

mother, he turns with relief to be the man-of-action, un-inhibited any more by religious motives. It is the last of the three *rôles* in which the Elizabethan hero liked to see himself: —Eremite, Politician, Man-of-Action.

The vanity of heroic action is shown up in the graveyard scene, prior to the entry of Ophelia's body. Hamlet's meditation is obviously based on some book of divinity. Reflections on the despair of Cain, the frustration of Alexander, the decomposition of Pompey and Caesar, are all in Persons, along with many other passages like the following:

> Where are now all those Emperours, those Kings, those Princes and Prelates, which rejoiced so much once at their own advancement? Where are they now, I say? Who talketh or thinketh of them? Are they not forgotten and cast into their graves long ago? And do not men boldly walk over their heads now, whose faces might not be looked on without fear in their lives? What then have their dignities done them good?
>
> Where are all my coaches and horses, wherewith I was wont to make so goodly a show: the caps and knees of people accustomed to honour me: the troops of suitors following me? Where are all my daliances and tricks of love: all my pleasant musick: all my gorgeous buildings: all my costly feasts and banquetings? And above all other, where are now my dear and sweet friends, who seemed they would never have forsaken me?
>
> Let the soul depart but one half hour from the body, and this loving face is ugly to look on: let it ly but two days in the grave, or above ground dead, and those who were so earnestly in love with it before, will scarce abide to behold or to come near it. And if none of these

---

the world and the flesh, and having failed, really, to redeem, his mother, he cries to the Ghost, sadly but irrevocably:

> Do not look upon me,
> Lest with this piteous action you convert
> My stern effects. (III. iv. 126–8)

The fading-out of the Ghost coincides with a fading-out of belief in any kind of revealed religion. And here, I think, is where the political arena of Acts I and IV dovetails into the psychological arena of Acts II and III. Knitting together most of the psychological explanations of Hamlet's distress—and not contradicting them—there is the crisis of a loss of Faith and spiritual moorings.

The thesis I am putting forward is that the Ghost, in the mind of many of Shakespeare's audience, would inevitably recall the Old Religion, with its doctrinal, psychological, *and* political implications. The mood he would be playing on would be the two-way one: a nostalgia for the ritual and reverence of the Old Religion, coupled with a revulsion for its positive discipline.

things happen unto it: yet quickly cometh on old age, which riveleth the skin, draweth in the eyes, setteth out the teeth, and so disfigureth the whole visage, as it becometh more contemptible and horrible now, than ever it was beautiful and alluring before.

And the speech of the skull:

I have been as lusty, jocund and frolick, as thou art at this present: I have been as proud and vain of my stature, beauty, hair, skin, agility, and nimblenesse, and of other qualities and decking up of my body, as thou has ever been, that now lookest upon me with disdain and contempt, and shortly thou shalt be what I am now: that is to say, a dried skull, bones without flesh, mouth without tongue, ear-holes without hearing, eye-pits without sight, brows without brains, and head without sense or feeling. The soul that was wont to quicken me, and give life to all, hath long ago abandoned me, and left me to be the food of worms . . .

Although I am not anxious to show that the *Christian Directory* was actually used by Shakespeare, yet there is a curiously close parallel with *King Lear*, (III. iv. 105–10). Lear is apostrophising naked man:

Is man no more than this? Consider him well. Thou ow'st the worm no silk, the beast no hide, the sheep no wool, the cat no perfume. Ha! here's three on's are sophisticated! Thou art the thing itself . . . Off, off, you lendings!

Persons has:

We rob and spoil all sorts of creatures upon earth, to cover our backs and adorn our bodies. From one we take his wooll: from another his skinne: from another his hair and furre: and from other their very excrements as the silk which is nothing else but the excrement of worms . . . When Cats-dung does smell in our garments, we would have men think that we send forth sweet odour from ourselves. And thus (as the Prophet saith) we pass our days in vanity, and do not perceive our own extreme folly.

However, the only conclusion I wish to draw is that Hamlet *has been* dipped deep in some book of Divinity. *Has been*: for what we witness in Acts II and III is the breakdown of a high spiritual purpose, caused by being "lapsed in time and passion": entangled, that is, by the need for "practising" politics, and by the failure of Grace to transform concupiscence.

This fits in with the previous batch of references; and both are suitable to what I conceive to be the tragic theme of the play. The theme is the quasi-Orestean conflict between the influences of a dead father and of a living mother, and of the spiritual forces which they represent.

The end is nostalgia. Hamlet has died a martyr for no known cause. Horatio throws in a merciful line recalling that moment in the forbidden ritual when the choir sings, as the bearers lift the body from the transept: *In Paradisum deducant te Angeli*. In a way the whole play is transformed:

> Good night, sweet prince,
> And flights of angels sing thee to thy rest. (V. ii. 373–4)

NOTE ON POLITICS

Many readers will reject with impatience the suggestion—not a new one—that the Ghost's demand for vengeance is a reflection of the political unrest of the time. Certainly—though Polonius is a fairly obvious caricature of Burleigh—no strict historical parallel should be pressed. But that does not mean that one can ignore the threat of the "impostume," lurking on the outskirts of *Hamlet* as it lurked in the minds of Englishmen at the opening of the seventeenth century. Compare Decker's *The Wonderfull Yeare 1603*: "The great impostume has drawn even to a head."

It is also true that in the main body of the play, Acts II and III, Hamlet's revenge is seen as a private affair. But the political uneasiness stressed in Act I, returns quite noticably in Act IV. Hamlet's revenge is conceived, albeit reluctantly, in Act I, and concluded in Act V as a "publique revenge"—to use Bacon's phrase.

An audience of the time would fully have shared Hamlet's revulsion from the idea of public revenge—though not for quite the same reason. Public revenge meant foreign intervention. Foreign intervention, both in Act I and in IV and V, is Young Fortinbras. There is no word of Hamlet having "strength and means" to execute his public revenge, *until* the entry of Fortinbras's army in IV. iv. Politically conscious as it was, the audience would already be asking: what dramatic use was going to be made of the "shark'd up list of lawless resolutes." Foreign intervention was inseparable from the Catholic-Protestant controversy. This last element is essential in the vague but formidable picture of the Old Religion that would be conjured up by the Ghost.

To the objection that Shakespeare would never have dared to trifle thus with the loyalty of an Elizabethan audience, the answer is that the play as we know it was presented to a *Jacobean* audience. Fortinbras's intervention might be seen as the accession of James. James not only healed the wounds opened by the Essex revolt, but he, rather unexpectedly, took a firm anti-Catholic stand.

No requiem for old Hamlet?

IN an article entitled "The Ghost in *HAMLET*, a Catholic Linchpin?"[1] Mr Roy Battenhouse contends that the Ghost as drawn by Shakespeare is a pagan shade in a pagan context, and as such it would have been received by Shakespeare's audience. The author is led naturally in the course of his article to attack Professor Dover Wilson's position, that the Ghost is "a Catholic Ghost"; and against him, and others, he lists seven reasons.

A good deal of logomachy may be avoided if one recalls two things. First, Dover Wilson did not exclude an element of doubt from the Ghost's Catholic credentials; such an element is essential to the plot. Dover Wilson's theory, as I understood it, was that the overall impression given is that of a soul from Purgatory, and yet there is sufficient doubt to keep the audience guessing. Secondly, Dover Wilson did not conceive the Ghost as fitted out to the prescriptions of St Thomas Aquinas and the Council of Trent, but as fitting in with the average Catholic notions of the day. These notions were inevitably tinged with "paganism" (though the word is misleading,) both by accretions from renaissance classicism, and, even more, by the survival of an ancient pre-Christian background. A modern Catholic writer on Purgatory has gone so far as to say:

> The sombre demonism which runs amuk in nearly all the descriptions of Purgatory of bygone times does not redound to the credit of those ages; it belongs to the same category as the belief in witchcraft which disgraced past centuries.[2]

Mr Battenhouse is on insecure ground when he complains that the Ghost's description of Purgatory sounds more like

[1] *Studies in Philology*, April 1951, Washington.
[2] Bartmann: *Purgatory* (London, 1936), p. xv.

Hell. In the ancient descriptions, still current among Elizabethan Catholics, the physical pains of Purgatory were exactly the same as those of Hell, except in point of duration.

Mr Battenhouse's first positive reason has more force. If the Ghost were a soul from Purgatory, it would revisit earth for only two reasons: first, to solicit prayers, secondly, to issue a warning against sin. The Ghost's "Pity me not" is taken as a refusal to ask for prayers. But is it not rather a postponement of the first task in favour of the second? The Ghost has first to make clear the heinous sin which has to be "revenged" (i.e. wiped out) in order that Denmark may be cleansed. Having done that, he *does* ask for prayers, briefly, and like a soldier, but very impressively. He says "remember me" and the words echo and re-echo in Hamlet's soul more than any others. Their effect is to rouse in him the most intense pity, and a desire for prayer. "For my own poor part, look you, I'll go pray." (I. v. 131–2.) And so he does, *teste Polonio*: he ruins his health by fasting and vigil. All this is as it should be. Mr Battenhouse does not strengthen his case by his argument (p. 164) that if the Ghost were a soul from Purgatory it would approve of fasting, whereas, about "fasting in fires," it says "O, horrible!" The exclamation-mark, here, refers to the argument. Is it necessary to point out that the words, "O, horrible, etc." express Catholic horror at death without the Sacraments?

Mr Battenhouse's second reason is his big gun. A soul from Purgatory should inculcate humility and forgiveness; but the Ghost incites to hatred and to a revenge that must lead to murder. There is much force in this argument, and I agree with Mr Battenhouse that some at least among the audience would have felt shocked by this demand of the Ghost. The shock would be enough to weaken, but not to obliterate, the over-all impression of the Ghost as a soul from Purgatory. It must be remembered that the word "revenge" had a pefectly proper purgatorial sense. Here are two quotations from books of the day on Purgatory, one a very popular work by Father Persons, the other by Cardinal Allen. The Persons quotation is a long one, but it is useful also as an example of horrific Catholic descriptions of Purgatory:

And the same S. Austen in another place expoundeth yet further the words of the said Apostle in this manner. "They which have done things worthy of temporall punishment must passe through a fiery river, and most horrible shallows of burning flames . . . And look how much matter there is left in their sinnes, so long must they stick in passing through; how much the fault requireth, so much all the punishment of this fire revenge.[1]

"And because the word of God doth compare the soule of a sinner to a pot of brasse, saying, 'Put the pot empty upon the coals untill all the rust be melted off': therefore in this fire all idle speeches, all filthy cogitations, all light sins shall boil out and consume, which by a short way might have been separated from the soul in this life, by alms and tears.' Hitherto S. Austen."

"Revenge" here means "purge"; and the context is eminently suitable to the Ghost—

> Confin'd to fast in fires,
> Till the foul crimes done in my days of nature
> Are burnt and purg'd away. (I. iv. 10–12)

The passage in Cardinal Allen's book is clearer. He is speaking of the spiritual body:

To the newness whereof, the very elements that before answered it in qualities of corruption shall be perfectly by fire reformed and serve in beauty and incorruption eternal. If sin then be so revenged and thoroughly tried out of man's body, and all corruption out of these elements, for the glory of that new and eternal kingdom, shall we doubt of God's justice in the perfect revenge of sin in the soul, or purifying that nature which, as it was most corrupted and was the very seat of sin, so namely appertaineth to the company of angels and glory everlasting?[2]

Here again the meaning of revenge is that of purifying or purging the effects of sin. It must be remembered, also, that nowhere does the Ghost advocate assassination or even violence. On the contrary, it says:

> But howsoever thou pursuest this act,
> Taint not thy mind nor let thy soul contrive
> (I. v. 84–5)

—a most Christian sentiment. Mr Battenhouse explains away "Taint not thy soul," by saying that it cannot be a prohibition of murder, because if it were the Ghost would not be in the

---

[1] Persons: *Christian Directory* (1650 Edition), p. 365.
[2] Allen: *A Defense of Purgatory* (Antwerp, 1565), p. 592.

Senecan tradition of Kyd. This is the form of argument known, I believe, as a *petitio principii*.

All the same there *is* force in the argument, and there is something of the Senecan Ghost in old Hamlet. Since his original was presumably a Senecan ghost, it would be surprising if there were not. But what is more surprising is that so much Catholic atmosphere should have been worked in. The result is, perhaps, one of the reasons why Professor Tillyard, following Mr Traversi, calls *Hamlet* a "Problem Play."[1]

As to the further argument that young Hamlet interprets "revenge" as "assassination"—*that* is an entirely different question, and one that goes right to the heart of the problem. Two considerations must suffice. (a) Professor Tillyard, without *parti pris* in this matter, sees the Ghost's main preoccupation as the redemption of Gertrude. (b) when Hamlet does decide on active measures against Claudius, he does so at a time when the Ghost has ceased to influence his actions. This last point is important. There is a clear psychological connection between the Ghost's visitation and Hamlet's desire for prayer but there is no such connection between the Ghost's visitation and Hamlet's plans to overthrow Claudius. A lot of things happen in between.

Mr Battenhouse's third reason is his last effective shot. It is that the Ghost's attitude to Claudius and to Gertrude shows a resentment and *amour-propre* more consonant with a Senecan shade than with a Holy Soul. There is not much in this, taken by itself, but it does add cumulative force to the two points already made—and Mr Battenhouse's argument is of a cumulative nature. In reply, without wishing to be pedantic, one might point out that the Ghost's execration of Claudius and praise of himself is objective evidence incidental to his main purpose: to incite his son to redeem Gertrude—"O Hamlet, what a falling-off was there!" This form of argument opens the way to endless logomachy ("But Hamlet knew all that beforehand, etc."). I do not wish to crab a spontaneous impression by niggling manipulation of the text. No, I see

[1] E. M. W. Tillyard, *Shakespeare's Problem Plays*, (London, Chatto & Windus, 1950).

Mr Battenhouse's point, but I have a genuine spontaneous impression that cancels its effect in my mind. It is that the Ghost is much more of a Holy Soul when it appears in Gertrude's bed-chamber. Shakespeare seems quite rightly, to have conceived purgation as a process. The Ghost is "gracious" this time, not hideous; its supernatural power is gentler and more sublime:

> His form and cause conjoined,
> Preaching to stones, would make them capable.
> (III. iv. 125-6)

It betokens only tender solicitude for Gertrude's soul, and sad reproach to Hamlet for the course he has embarked on. That is why Hamlet cries:

> Do not look upon me;
> Lest with this piteous action you convert
> My stern effects. (III. iv. 126-8)

For Hamlet has set himself to out-machiavel his machiavellian enemies. He has become involved in what Mr J. F. Danby has called "the problem of the good man in a bad society."[1] Unless one is a saint, or a maniac, or a hypocrite, the devout practice of religion is a heavy clog of a successful *coup d'état*, for "conscience doth make cowards of as all." The equivocal attitude of the Ghost—seeming to incite Hamlet to a certain end, and then seeming to disapprove the means to the end—is analogous with the part played by religion in the political strife of the period. It forms an integral knot in the Hamlet problem which Mr Battenhouse's Gordian methods will not solve. But lest I also be accused of *petitio principii*, I have relied on the text and not on theories to answer his difficulties.

Mr Battenhouse's remaining reasons may be briefly dealt with.

The Fourth—Private revelations are contrary to Catholic Doctrine? It is true that the Council of Trent in its last session (1563) disapproved of private revelations as arguments for Purgatory. But they died hard. Lessius, a post-Tridentine theologian who had considerable indirect influence on Elizabethan Catholics, makes extensive use of private revelations

[1] J. F. Danby, *Shakespeare's Doctrine and Nature*, 1949.

48

in a treatise on Purgatory, which, incidentally contains one
of the most horrific descriptions on record:

> flammis undique corpus eius usque
> ad viscera depascentibus.

The Fifth—Hamlet never accepted the Ghost as a soul from
Purgatory? He did, and then again he didn't. That is one of
Dover Wilson's main points. "Yes, by Saint Patrick," can
have only one significance. The terrible other-worldy sights
seen in the "purgatory" of Lough Dearg were talked about
in England as early as 1571, when Campion in his *Historie of
Ireland* described the place—"because I would be discharged
of my readers' expectation." They must have been even
better known in 1600, after so many playgoers had served in
Ulster. As to the cellarage scene, Dover Wilson has his own
explanation; but the idea of echoing elements transmitting
a supernatural message is found in writings of the Fathers.
The Sixth—Horatio and Marcellus never accepted the Ghost
as a soul from Purgatory? Horatio and Marcellus were, very
naturally, intent on having as little as possible to do with the
apparition, whatever it was. There is nothing demonstrably
pagan about that. Some of Horatio's lines come straight out
of the Roman Liturgy. It is these that Mr Battenhouse
regards as "deceptively inbellished with some superstitious
touches of nominal Christianity?" Why "deceptively?" What
with angels, requiems, sacraments, and saints, Shakespeare
seems to have carried the deception rather far. To say that
the pagan ghost is effectively disguised as a Catholic, may
turn out not very different in the end from saying that the
Catholic ghost has a pagan tincture.

In fact Mr Battenhouse's seventh and last reason clinches
this point against himself rather neatly. In order to negate
the Ghost's obvious references to temporal punishment after
death, he says that the pagans also had the idea of Purgatory.
He quotes, interestingly, William Fulke who urged this point
against Cardinal Allen's book. In extenuation of the Catholic
teaching, Mr Battenhouse adds (p. 192):

> It would not be surprising if pagan notions became blurred with
> Christian in popular thinking.

But the obvious inference from these kindly words is that one would expect a Catholic ghost to be tinged with "paganism."

What really persuades people that the Ghost is a Catholic ghost is its appalled horror at having to die suddenly without the Last Sacraments. Mr Battenhouse's evasion of this point borders on the puerile. He says that Hamlet uses a Catholic oath, but this does not prove he was a Catholic; he was in fact a Protestant. (*Not* a pagan, then, Mr Battenhouse?) Similarly, the Ghost talks about Catholic Sacraments, but this does not prove he was a Catholic; he was in fact a pagan. Does one have to insist that a Catholic oath shows, at most, a Catholic inclination, whereas only a believing Catholic would desire the Last Sacraments on his death-bed?

As to young Hamlet's religious views, the impression that one gets is that they were typically Elizabethan; he was a conforming Protestant, with Catholic inclinations counter-balanced by an increasing tendency to scepticism—a man, for example, like Ferdinando Lord Strange, or Shakespeare himself—or like Southampton or Mountjoy, whose fathers were devout Catholics.

Mr Battenhouse has made out a good case that Shakespeare views his ghost from a "post-Christian" standpoint. But even here one must be careful of too rigid a line between Christian and "post-Christian"; the age was a fluid one and the man was man, not a packet of labels. Mr Battenhouse's article is a useful reminder that in *Hamlet*, as far as we are concerned, Shakespeare deals in impressions, rather than in constructions; and with impressions we must be content. The overall impression, which he has not seriously weakened, is that the Ghost is a Catholic ghost purporting to come from Purgatory.

The failure of the English Inquisition

An Incident of 1588

THE qualities that make a people free and high-spirited against oppression do not, undiluted, guarantee that *within* its borders there will be liberty of conscience and "toleration" in the modern usage. As an example one might cite the popular support of the Spanish Inquisition; and one might also glance interrogatively, but without saying anything, at the "Loyalty Boards" in the United States today.

The diluted qualities that do guarantee toleration are not easy to describe. But they are fairly easy to envisage, because they appear with such rounded completeness in the English character: in the English character, that is, as moulded by the centuries; for a sense of history, conscious or not, is one certain element in guaranteeing toleration. It may be of interest, therefore, to consider a moment in our history when an English Inquisition, as a more or less popular institution, came very near to establishing itself.

It was in the summer of 1588. The Privy Council, which at that very busy moment meant virtually Lord Burghley, had consulted the Crown lawyers about framing a loyalty-test which should go deeper than anything attempted before. On 20 July, the very day that the Armada was sighted off the Lizard, the lawyers sent their reply. In order to appreciate this reply, one must consider some of the events that had gone before.

Early in the year, the leading Catholic knights and squires had been interned, first at Ely, and later in ten or twelve "concentration-camps" throughout the country. The point is of some importance; it reminds one that the minority that was being proceded against did not consist of alien outcasts.

These "internees" had been the pillars of traditional loyalty in their parishes or counties.

For the next six months, however, an uneasy lull prevailed. The Armada, after two false starts, put back to port in May. There were rumours that the death of Santa Cruz had taken the heart out of the expedition. Queen Elizabeth opened negotiations with the Prince of Parma who was reported to have the gravest doubts of success. The English admiral, Lord Howard, who was chafing to repeat Drake's exploit at Cadiz, was ordered not to stir beyond the Channel. The cloudy peace, or "cold war," seemed likely to continue indefinitely, when, about midsummer, suddenly and dramatically, things began to happen.

In June, the English spy-service in the Netherlands, by a smart piece of work, secured a copy of a broadside *Declaration* being printed in English at Antwerp for distribution if the Spanish army were to land. It was by Cardinal Allen: a summary of his short book, the *Admonition*, which he had written the previous April at the instance of Philip of Spain. Denouncing Elizabeth in harsh terms as a female tyrant unguided by moral principles, it proclaimed that King Philip was to give effect to the decree of excommunication which previous Pontiffs had been unable to execute; that England was not to be subjugated but set free; and that all should rally to the Prince of Parma on his landing.

It was not intended for publication except in the event of Parma's landing in force, and in that event, presumably, as a safeguard for Catholics against a possible "Spanish Fury." But by 12 June a copy of Allen's book was in Burghley's hands, and a copy also of the broadside *Declaration* reached him before the 24th.

On 22 June the die was cast. Howard got the orders he was longing for; he set sail and, with a little more luck, would have crippled the Armada as it lay along the coast of Biscay. As it was, he had to return and await its slow arrival in the Channel. In the meantime, while most of the other Councillors were engaged in fervent preparations by land, Lord Burghley had been meditating how to make the best use of the *Declaration* that had come into his hands.

In spite of the crisis, his thoughts moved along familiar lines. As early as 1583 he had urged the Queen to frame an oath of allegiance that would split the Catholics on the hypothetical issue of what they would do if a Papal army were to land in England:

> Hereof this commodity would ensue. That those papists (as I think most papists would) that should take this oath, would be divided from the great mutual confidence that now is betwixt the Pope and them by reason of their afflictions for him. And such priests as would refuse that oath no tongue could say for shame that they suffered for religion if they did suffer.[1]

The majority, as he hoped, would lose the link with Rome which was the source of their spiritual strength, while the minority could be exterminated, literally or otherwise, by popular acclamation without undue scandal. The moment for perfecting this policy seemed now at hand. But with his eye on foreign opinion, he could not resist giving an extra twist to it. He wrote to Walsingham on 12 June:

> I could wish some expert learned man would feign an answer as from a number of Catholics that notwithstanding their evil contentment for Religion should profess their obedience and promise with their lives and power against all strange forces offering to land in this realm. And to advertise the Cardinal that he is deceived in his opinion to think that any noble man in this land or any Gentleman of possession will favour the invasion of the realm. And that such a rash writing may give cause of danger of life to all that are reputed Catholics, specially to all recusants.[2]

He was proposing to praise the leading Catholics, who were all interned, for their unhesitating loyalty; and at the same time he was contemplating the possibility of having them all massacred. It might be unfair to press his words—which were written understandably, as he said, "in choler"—if it were not that they correspond with the policy which he had outlined five years before and which he afterwards tried to carry out in cold blood.

The first part of his proposal, the counterfeit answer from

---

[1] Burghley's authorship of this treatise has been questioned. But I have accepted its ascription to him in the Petyt MSS. (Series 538, Vol. xliii, f. 304 . . .).

[2] *S.P.D.*, Vol. ccxi, No. 15. Printed by Pollen in *C.R.S.*, Vol. xxi, p. 169.

the leading Catholics, was embarked on forthwith. It took shape as the famous *Letter . . . to . . . Mendoza* which has deceived historians down to the present day, though there are drafts of it in Burghley's hand among the Lansdowne manuscripts.

> Amongst infinite other errors, [as Pollen notes], the writer states that many copies of "The Bull" (*i.e.*, the *Declaration*) had been introduced into England. It was probably through this widely-spread letter, which was translated into foreign languages and circulated on the Continent, that the false idea of the Pope having again excommunicated Elizabeth was popularised among non-Catholics and anti-papalists.

The second part of his proposal, the preparation for a general massacre, was launched with the *Proclamation* of 1 July, "against bringing in Bulls from the See of Rome," which was particularly designed to rouse mob-fury.[1] The stress was on Rome, not on Spain. The Cardinal's *Declaration*, though it was kept secret, was described as a Bull issued with the Pope's spiritual authority.

It was not a Bull, as anyone could see who had a copy in his hands; and even as a Cardinal's pronouncement it lacked all binding force, since it was never promulgated. Burghley, however, could argue with reason that if it had been promulgated the Pope would have backed it up. This was sufficient; for it was his intention to catch the Catholics in a *hypothetical* dilemma, to make their guilt hang on their answer what they *would* have done *if* . . . the Pope with the plentitude of his spiritual power gave them orders to side with the invasion.

Thus was born the notorious "Bloody Question" in the form that Gerard remembered it put to him:

> If the Pope were to send over an army and declare that his only object was to bring back the kingdom to its Catholic allegiance—what would you do? And if he stated at the same time that there was no other way of re-establishing the Catholic faith, and commanded everyone by his apostolic authority to support him? Whose side would you be on—the Pope's or the Queen's?[2]

It was a question along these lines—as may be gathered from the lawyer's reply—that Burghley wanted to bring into

[1] Printed by Strype, *Annals*, iii, 2, 87–92 (1824).
[2] P. Caraman, *John Gerard*, p. 98.

54

English judicature. A Catholic was to be bound by law to answer, and if he could not answer "The Queen's," he convicted himself of High Treason. It should be remarked that the whole value of the question lay in the Catholics being people who, as Burghley put it in his own words, "make conscience of an oath."[1]

From a Catholic point of view, indeed, the question was a device to torture conscience rather than to test loyalty. But from the legal point of view, surely, its chief interest is that it condemned a man to death for secret thoughts which need never issue in an overt act of conspiracy. A further point is that it assumed the English system of law to be *inquisitorial*— a system, that is, in which it is for the accused to prove himself innocent, not for the prosecution to prove him guilty. It would be interesting, if one had the capacity, to discuss how far these two innovations had made practical headway during Tudor times, particularly in Elizabeth's reign. Such a discussion no doubt would bristle with difficulties even for an expert. But there was a third innovation closely allied to the foregoing, which it is easier to assess; and that was the increasing use of torture.

Torture had never been recognised in English Common Law. In the previous century it had come to be accepted as a part of extraordinary criminal procedure, exercisable by the royal prerogative. But in Elizabeth's reign it exceeded the bounds of civilised usage, even by the lax standards of contemporary Europe.

> In other countries [as Selden noted], it is used in judicature when there is a *semi-plena probatio*, a half-proof against a man; then to see if they can make it full, they rack him if he will not confess; but here in England they take a man and rack him, I do not know why nor when— not in time of judicature, but when somebody bids.[2]

[1] The play *Titus Andronicus* (about 1590) has an interesting confirmation of this common view of Catholics. The villain Aaron scoffs:
> Yet, for I know thou art religious
> And hast a thing within thee called conscience,
> With twenty popish tricks and ceremonies
> Which I have seen thee careful to observe,
> Therefore I urge thy oath.

[2] *Table Talk*, "Trial."

But what Selden criticised in Stuart times was only the waning residue of what had been a peak-period in Elizabeth's reign. What made the usage so terrible was that it could be delegated and sub-delegated without any recognised limitation, because it had no recognised existence. A general warrant of 1590 to Richard Topcliffe, endorsed for the Keeper of the common prison of Bridewell,[1] has these phrases: *"torture upon the wall . . . from time to time . . . as is usual. . . ."* Yet only three years earlier Harrison's *Description of England* had been re-issued containing the words: "Our gaolers are guilty of felony by an old law of the land if they torment any prisoner committed to their custody, for the revealing of his complices."

The danger, as in all encroachments of the executive, was that any law to check its worst excesses would at the same time acknowledge its existence as part of the system.

When one considers these various tendencies in the same direction—the tendency to take secret thoughts instead of overt acts as matter for trial—the tendency to assume guilt and to exact self-accusation instead of proof—the practical acquiescence in torture—and finally, what has already been mentioned at this juncture, the deliberate official instigation of popular fury—it does not seem too much to conclude that England was on the verge of accepting the worst evils of the Spanish Inquisition without the safeguards maintained by that body.

If that is so, then the reply of the lawyers to Lord Burghley may be taken as a crucial event in the history of English law.

But once again the text of the reply must be postponed for a moment while one considers the state of mind of the recusant English Catholics. Judged by political labels it was a complex state of mind; but psychologically it was a very simple one; and it was expressed in one simple sentence by Fr Henry Garnet in a letter to his General at Rome. He was describing the ruin of the Fitzherbert family by Topcliffe in July of that year, and how it coincided in time and place with the pardoning of a batch of hardened criminals "because in these troubled times the Queen has need of such men"; and

[1] *S.P.D.*, Vol. ccxxx, No. 57.

he added, "How happy she would be (and I would to God she were) if it were the other sort of men that she had need of."[1]

Their cruel dilemma has of course been blamed on Cardinal Allen's *Declaration*. But that is a superficial view, mistaking a mere occasion, and an undivulged one, for a cause. Their dilemma had been confronting them implicitly for a long time. As it became explicit they girded themselves to meet it as best they could in their state of ignorance. There was a consultation in London, and their decisions were circulated among as many recusants as possible, especially among those in the London gaols, who were nearly all awaiting trial by the Statute of 1585 which enacted the death-penalty for the saying or hearing of the Mass.

The gist of their decisions was: that they were to maintain their traditional loyalty, that they were to take evasive action on the Pope's temporal power, since its limits were still disputed among theologians, but that they were to maintain unshaken their attachment to the Mass. The evasive action would avail them nothing against the Bloody Question if relentlessly pressed. But, as things turned out, it was of great importance.

The reply to Burghley on 20 July came from Fleetwood, Recorder of London, who was considered one of the ablest lawyers of his day though he had been passed over for promotion, and from Egerton, the Solicitor-General, and it was signed in that order. Not at first sight a promising choice for Catholics. Egerton was an ex-recusant anxious to live down the fact. Fleetwood was well known for his rigorous enforcement of the Statute of '85 and his scathing gibes at "massing-priests." Yet there are indications that it was Fleetwood who was responsible for the stubborn core of the reply, which now at last is quoted:

> And albeit it cannot be otherwise presumed but that all such as will not dutifully clear themselves upon these questions, by professing their loyalty and obedience to her Majesty, are (at this time specially)

[1] Garnet to Aquaviva, 11 July and 29 October 1588, *Arch. Rom. S. J.*, *Fondo Gesuitico*, 651. Other letters from the same source, used in this article, are from Southwell to Aquaviva, 11 July and 31 August.

exceeding dangerous persons. *Yet* if they do either obstinately refuse to make any answer at all, or subtly (as many in like cases have heretofore done) excuse themselves that they are unlearned and ignorant and so not able to answer herein, or that they ought not to be examined of things future or to like effect: *Then* upon such manner of answer made by them, they are not comprehended directly within the compass of the law for any proceeding to be had against them in case of Treason or felony in respect of that their answer only, unless some other action drawing them in danger of the law may be proved against them.[1]

The answer was just the opposite of what Burghley wanted. "They should never have the honour to take any pretence of Martyrdom in England," he had written in 1583, for "that vice of obstinacy seems to the common people a divine constancy." But now he was back at the Statute of '85 which was a martyr-making Statute; it might please the extreme Protestants, but the majority of the nation, still vaguely Catholic at heart, had never liked it. To sweep away the recusants on a charge of aiding the enemy would have been quick and easy in the atmosphere of 1588, but to rake up evidence of sheltering priests or attending Mass was the reverse. The Government was faced with a private dilemma of its own: the legal verdict would not be popular, but the popular verdict was illegal.

The dilemma was solved in a way that seemed at first to nullify the value of Fleetwood's reply. The papers of the Crown advocate, Puckering, a political lawyer, show that in a list of forty-seven prisoners questioned between 14 and 20 August, their sentences (generally "*susp.*", *i.e.*, let him be hanged) have been written against their names before trial in terms of the Bloody Question; guilty, that is, if they had not agreed to take the Queen's part against the Pope under any circumstances. The prosecution was conducted on those lines, that the accused were Papal spies and Spanish agents. But the actual verdict was passed hurriedly on the charge of being or of aiding priests.[2]

As a short-term expedient this was successful. At the first batch of executions on 28 August, eight days after the Thanks-

---

[1] *S.P.D.*, Vol. ccxii, No. 70. Printed by Pollen, *C.R.S.*, Vol. v, p. 151.
[2] See Pollen, as before, pp. 154–5.

58

giving at St Paul's, the crowd duly chanted: "This priest for the Pope is hanged with a rope." But on the second day, 30 August, there was evidence of a revulsion of feeling. Other victims were taken outside London to be hanged elsewhere later on. But the total number of executions as a result of the Armada—thirty-three—was much less than at first had seemed likely.

The reason given in contemporary letters for this unexpected relief are interesting. The evidence for the formal verdict was often so hasty and inadequate that some of the judges on the bench protested. Among them—we learn from a letter of Garnet's—was Fleetwood. Moreover the mild and resolute answers of the Catholics on trial and their bearing on the scaffold had begun to make it plain that they were dying for the Mass, not for the Armada. There was one particular execution of a lady, Margaret Ward, well known for her charity, that was a mistake from a Government point of view. On the next occasion of a woman being condemned, Fleetwood took advantage of her sex and protested to the Queen, who issued a reprieve. This seems to have been the turn of the tide. Perhaps an additional cause was that as soon as the religious character of the persecution became apparent it ceased to have any value for Burghley who was filling the Continent with the spurious *Letter to Mendoza* about no Catholic in England suffering for religion merely.

Burghley had succeeded in creating for posterity the Myth in which the old religion figured as foreign tyranny and the brand-new Genevan one as traditional patriotism. Yet the pragmatic effects of his policy were not successful. As the sense of national well-being decayed and turned sour during the last fifteen years of Elizabeth's reign, the hacked root of Catholicism flowered—incredibly—and began to spread. They had still to endure ten years of torture by the Bloody Question, a persecution in which Topcliffe played the part of Torquemada, though he was the opposite of that worthy in character. Yet at the end of the reign they emerged in better shape than the Puritans who had seemed to be on the crest of the wave in 1587.

The Puritan parliamentarians are generally credited with

awakening the national conscience to the dangers that threatened Common law and the subject's liberty. But might it not be truer to say that the national conscience had been building itself up for a long time previously, and that what the Puritans did, by a political manoeuvre, was to scoop the pool—and then squander it?

An early instance of muffled anger at the use of torture was the trial of Robert Southwell in 1595. At that trial the prosecuting Attorney, Edward Coke, shouted at him across the court: "Mr Topcliffe has no need to go about to excuse the manner of his torturings. For think you that you will not be tortured? Yea, we will tear the hearts out of an hundred of your bodies."

Many years later the same Edward Coke, now a champion of liberty, uttered his famous sentence: "There is no law to warrant tortures in this land, nor can they be justified by any prescription, being so lately brought in."

It may be that the Catholic recusant contribution, both active and passive, to law and liberty has not received its due recognition.

Richard Topcliffe

"How comes it, then, that thou art out of hell?"
"Why, this is hell, nor am I out of it."
Marlowe's *Faustus*.

TOPCLIFFE is a nightmare temptation to the middle-aged failure. Here is a man who, by patiently adhering to the principle of evil, through years of disappointment, attained in the end to all that he had bargained for: luxury, adulation, and despotic power. His case is the more striking because he lacked all the intellectual and physical grace which, in Renaissance eyes, was essential to success. Intellectually, his most illustrious victim, Robert Southwell, summed him up: "I have found by experience that the man is not open to reason." Physically, he had a strong animal magnetism, which he traded on. The terror he sought to inspire was the superstitious terror that one feels of a wild beast: of flattened ears and dripping fangs, bristling fur and glaring eyes.

But it was only in his declining years that political recognition gave scope to this feral power. Extreme brutality to the helpless usually means an apprenticeship of extreme servility to the strong. Topcliffe's first appearance on the scene of public persecution is in the part of an applauding spectator. The occasion was the Queen's Progress through Norfolk in 1578. Elizabeth with her retinue had quartered herself unexpectedly on a Catholic gentleman named Rookwood. Topcliffe has described with gusto how Rookwood was compensated for his enforced hospitality. (I have had to alter his peculiar spelling so as to make it intelligible.)

Her excellent Majesty gave to Rookwood ordinary thanks for his bad house, and her fair hand to kiss. But my Lord Chamberlain, nobly and gravely understanding that Rookwood was excommunicated for Papistry, called him before him; demanded of him how he durst presume to attempt her real presence, he, unfit to accompany any Christian person; forthwith said he was fitter for a pair of stocks, commanded him out of the Court, and yet to attend her Council's pleasure; and at Norwich he was committed. And, to decipher the gent. to the full: a piece of plate being missed in the Court, and searched for in his hay house, in the hay rick such an image of our Lady was there found, as for greatness, for gayness, and workmanship, I never did see a match; and after a sort of country dances ended, in her Majesty's sight the idol was set behind the people, who avoided: She seemed rather a beast, raised upon a sudden from hell by conjuring, than the picture for whom it had been so often and so long abused. Her Majesty commanded it to the fire, which in her sight by the country folks was quickly done, to her content, and unspeakable joy of every one but some one or two who had sucked of the idol's poisoned milk.

Topcliffe's enthusiastic approval of the scene was ominous. Henceforth, he was to figure more and more as a sort of grisly backside to the fair, pompous frontage of Elizabeth's Court. The stench of his torture-house was to pervade the Royal Presence until "all the perfumes of Arabia will not sweeten this little hand."

In 1580 the sudden revival of Catholic fervour meant intensified persecution. The rack-master boasted that he had stretched one of Campion's companions a foot longer than God made him. That must have struck a tremulous chord of emulation in Topcliffe's breast. In 1581 he appeared on Burleigh's pay-roll as an official pursuivant. In 1582 he got his first assighment: to track down Campion's publications. He was then fifty years of age—almost an old man by Elizabethan standards. What had he been doing with the best years of his life?

Very little is known of his career before that date. In a letter of 1595, he says that he is now sixty-three years old, and that his home was Somerley in Lincolnshire. He was born, therefore, in 1532. His father was Robert Topcliffe of Somerley, a country gentleman of ancient lineage. This would indicate that Richard Topcliffe was baptized and educated as a Catholic. But the all-important details of his childhood are unknown to us. He may, of course, have been beaten and starved in infancy, and this would account for his indoctrination with cruelty and greed. But there is no reason to suppose that he was. Perhaps public events may have done something to shape his outlook on life. He tells us in one letter, quite candidly, that his guiding principle from earliest years was: *indignatio principis mors est*. At the age of five he heard the tramp of the peasantry and chivalry of the North in arms for the Old Religion with the banner of the Five Wounds. By medieval standards that rally was invincible. But the King tricked them with fair promises, tripped them when their backs were turned, and then hacked them on the ground with such relentless butchery that all men knew that a new order of morality was now in force. Shortly after, came the dissolution of the Greater Monasteries; and the King's Servants crowded round for the spoils. It was a clear case of the triumph of fraud and violence over valour and simplicity. Richard Topcliffe must have grown up in the firm belief that Henry VIII was God, and that God rewarded the evil deeds of men better than the good ones.

The seed thus planted would have flourished in the Inns of Court where he spent the usual University years. To a brash, ambitious and rather thick-headed young man, whose spiritual life had been choked by self-indulgence, the garbled maxims of Machiavelli must have seemed like a revelation. Old fools told you that happiness was the reward for painfully encouraging your good impulses and suppressing the bad; whereas, to the enlightened, the truth was exactly the opposite; happiness—that is, prosperity—resulted from the skilful use of man's impulse to evil. As he watched the crowds, in the reign of Edward VI, tearing and spoiling the Church treasures, he must have felt relief that he was no longer a Catholic, and supreme contempt for those "God Almighty's fools" who put their trust in these "idolls." The idols were ruining those who reverenced them and rewarding their destroyers. In this happy blend of rationalism and superstition, Topcliffe, at the age of twenty-one, must have faced the future with confidence. But in 1533 Mary acceded, and the idols returned. *Indignatio principis mors est*. Topcliffe lay low. He escaped attention during Mary's reign. But equally he escaped recognition when Elizabeth succeeded. Elizabeth was so obviously Henry VIII's daughter that Topcliffe must have longed for recognition from this feminine reincarnation of his childhood's dream. Young sparks with handsome legs, half-papists too some of them, shouldered and pushed their way past him. The barren years that followed, the years between twenty-five and forty, that should have been so fruitful, must have given Topcliffe a very jagged temper.

But in 1569, once more there came the tramp of the peasantry and chivalry of the North. Topcliffe had to make a decision. In the great hand-out of 1536, his father had got nothing, either because he was too honest or too timid. Richard Topcliffe was determined not to make the same mistake. He stuck boldly to his principle: *indignatio principis mors est*, and was justified. The rising collapsed, and in the spoliation that followed, he petitioned for the lands of Richard Norton the standard-bearer. He must have got something, for he speaks later of "Lynton, a town sometimes old Richard Norton's, the rebel in the North, now the Queen majesty's and under the charge and rule of Richard Topcliffe her Majesty's Servant." In connection, possibly, with this step-up, he was returned as member for Beverley to the Parliament of 1572.

He belonged, now, at the age of forty, to that select band of country gentlemen whom Professor Neale has described with such warm sympathy in his *Elizabethan House of Commons*. Since the House was mainly concerned with increasing the penal laws, he must have been a most suitable member. However, according to Professor Neale, the rewards of a member of parliament were mainly of a social nature:

A matchless attraction it was to be in London at this time; to be "of the parliament"; to move on the fringe of the Court, marvelling at its fashions and splendours; to see and hear the Queen; perchance to kiss her hand.

Perchance; all the same, some more solid emolument would have been welcome. He had "to move on the fringe of the Court" for ten years more before he appeared on Burleigh's pay-roll. His continued presence at Court argues some personal favour with the Queen; but the appointment of 1582, though it carried the title of "Her Majesty's Servant," was hardly more than that of a superior catch-pole.

In the years that followed, as the shadow of the Armada

64

drew nearer, he was promoted from the office of catch-pole to that of torturer and prober of minds. His associates were Richard Young and, a mere stripling, Francis Bacon. Their job was, "according to their good discretions," to administer the "Bloody Question" to priests and laymen. Bacon must have found this hanging around the rack, in the atmosphere of blood and vomit, a most irksome path to preferment. Not so Topcliffe; custom could not stale for him its infinite variety; and in his later days of despotic power, he still liked to conduct his inquiries personally. But he does not seem to have been much good at probing minds. In one of his windy reports to the Privy Council, he can only give his own opinions:

> . . . albeit they speak fair yet they seem to carry foul and traitorous hearts, and if they hurt not, it is not for want of will to attempt it, but for lack of force to accomplish it.

In another, he just changes the secretary's original "he will not side *against* the Queen" to "he will not side *with* the Queen . . ." Topcliffe was Burleigh's protégé. It may be conjecture that he did not cut much ice with Sir Francis Walsingham. Walsingham could twist the facts when he wanted to, but he wanted to have the facts first before he twisted them; he preferred a more detached, less fervid type of rogue. In the delicate affair of the Babington Plot, Topcliffe played no part. When mental torture was required, Richard Young was far more successful. He became "Justice Young." Topcliffe remained a bludgeon without a handle.

As if suspecting that promotion was unlikely under Walsingham, he began negotiations for his private advancement. The ancient Catholic family of the Fitzherbert contained one black sheep. Young Fitzherbert, having lost faith, morals, and money, was ready to go any length to oust his father and uncle from their estates. He came under Topcliffe's thumb, and "entered into bonds to give three thousand pounds unto Topcliffe if he would persecute his father and uncle to death." Accordingly, in 1588, three priests were trapped by treachery in the Fitzherbert house of Padley; they and almost all the Fitzherbert family were condemned and disposed of, either by execution or by gaol-fever. It only remained for Topcliffe to get a stranglehold on the young Fitzherbert, and then enjoy both the bribe and the estates. In 1589, Thomas Fitzherbert, for his own security, made over the house and estate of Padley to Richard Topcliffe. Honourable leisure seemed in sight.

But in 1590 an event occurred which opened a totally new chapter in Topcliffe's life, and in the history of crime. In April 1590, Sir Francis Walsingham died. Walsingham is rightly regarded as one of the worst enemies of the Faith; yet he had a certain grim sense of propriety. He would never have allowed a private citizen, a mere agent, to take the law uncontrollably into his own hands. So far, legal persuasion (which included ordinary racking), propaganda and pauperisation had failed to stem the purely spiritual resurgence of Catholicism. In the highest quarters a change of policy was decided on. Let them see what unlimited bludgeoning would do. Topcliffe was the man; he had no brains, but he had a filthy imagination. He was the Queen's choice. To the Queen he made his private reports, modifying them jocosely to suit her humour. When Southwell the poet was hung by the hands with spikes against his wrists, and his feet tied behind him clear of the ground, permission for this had been coaxed from the Queen in the course of a garrulous and chatty letter to her:

> To stand against the wall, his feet standing upon the ground, and his hands but as high as he can reach against the wall, like a Trick at Trenchmore,[1] will enforce him to tell all.

From 1590 onwards, Bridewell was put at the disposal of Young and Topcliffe, with Topcliffe as the senior partner. Bridewell was the prison, founded by Edward VI, for strumpets, rioters, and vagabonds. Promiscuity, whippings, nakedness, and shameful postures on the treadmill, were there the daily bread. Annexed to Bridewell, Topcliffe and Young had a private house which only they and their victims were allowed to enter. Between this house and Bridewell, the Faith had to be crushed.

It was some time before the Catholics realised that there

---

[1] Trenchmore was a skittish country dance.

was no appeal beyond Topcliffe. He was spy and sergeant, judge and counsel, warder and executioner, all in one. In 1591, a Yorkshire gentleman, Bryan Lacy, was guarding the door of Swithin Wells's house to enable a priest to finish Mass. In the scuffle that followed, a pursuivant was thrown from the top of the stairs to the bottom and received a bloody coxcomb. It was Topcliffe! One could dwell more pleasurably on this incident, if it were not for the sequel: "Bryan Lacy, a Yorkshire man, was pitifully tortured at Bridewell as himself declared at the time of his execution."

It says much for Bridewell that even Robert Southwell, who longed for martyrdom and had steeled himself to all its varieties, could write: "This is the one place that all we Catholics tremble at, where Topcliffe and Young, butchers, have unlimited liberty to torture."

When the blank wall of Topcliffe's omnipotence became obvious, one of its victims tried to undermine it by guile. Thomas Pormort was an acute young man, with ideas of his own and unflinching determination. He feigned compliance with Topcliffe. Yes, there were secrets that he knew, but he was afraid of offending people in high places—his god-father, Archbishop Whitgift, for instance. Topcliffe bridled; the scent of garbage called to him irresistibly. He assured Pormort that he need have no fear:

> That he did not care for the Council, for that he had his authority from her Majesty. That the Archbishop of Canterbury was a fitter Counsellor in the kitchen among wenches than in a Prince's court. . . . Item, Topcliffe offered him liberty, if he would say that he was a bastard of the Archbishop's of Canterbury.

Having thus unbuttoned himself, Topcliffe confided to Pormort odious details of the extent of his familiarity with the Queen, concluding:

> That he is so familiar with her that when he pleaseth to speak with her he may take her away from any company, and that she is as pleasant with everyone that she doth love.

In putting these gross distortions on paper,[1] Pormort did not mean to accuse the Queen, their victim, but Topcliffe,

[1] For the authority of this paper, cf. *Catholic Record Society*, vol. v, p. 209.

their author. The paper circulated among the Privy Councillors, and produced an effect. Pormort, at his execution, "was enforced to stand in his shirt almost two hours on the ladder, in Lent time upon a very cold day, when Topcliffe still urged him to deny the words, but *he would not*."

That was in 1592. In the previous year, a more orthodox attempt to rouse the Queen had been made by Robert Southwell. He had friends at Court, and knew of the public disgust with Topcliffe. In his *Humble Supplication* he credited the Queen with all the royal virtues, and assumed that if she knew what was going on, she would put a stop to it. Every detail in his description of Bridewell was a fact of bitter experience. The *Dictionary of National Biography*, on Topcliffe, observes: "The account of his cruel treatment of Southwell would be incredible, if it were not confirmed by admissions in his own handwriting."

Southwell knew of what he wrote:

> Some are hanged by the hands eight or nine hours, yea twelve hours together, till not only their wits but even their senses fail them; and when the soul (weary of so painful an harbour) is ready to depart, then they apply cruel comforts, and revive us only to martyr us with more deaths; for eftsoons they hang us in the same manner, trying our ears with such questions which either we cannot because we know not, or without damning of our souls we may not suffice. Some are whipped naked so long and with such excess that our enemies, unwilling to give constancy the right name, said that no man without the help of the devil could with such undauntedness suffer so much. Some, besides their torments, have been continually bobbed and clogged many weeks together, pined in their diet, consumed with vermin, and almost stifled with stench, and kept from sleep till they were past the use of reason, and then examined upon the advantage, when they could scarce give an account of their own names. Some have been tortured in those parts that it is almost a torture to Christian ears to hear it—let it be then judged what it was to chaste and modest men to endure it. . . . Some with instruments have been rolled up together like a ball, and so crushed that the blood sprouted out at diverse parts of their bodies.

Lest a blacker picture of Elizabethan England should be formed than of Nazi Germany, it should be added that the public scenes in Bridewell caused such scandal that, from 1592 onwards, they were confined exclusively to Topcliffe's private house. From its interior no news transpired except what Topcliffe cared to boast about:

As to the other, a man very gentle and of great penances, Topcliffe stated at Court on the very day that he martyred him that he thought he had done the Queen a better service that morning than he had for many a day before, for he had ridded the Queen of a Papist hypocrite, one who fasted more and prayed longer than any other in Europe.

"Mr Topcliffe hath waited on Her Majesty," wrote the Earl of Huntingdon, in February 1594, anxious for the approval of so important an emissary. The Ape, who had cavorted so long around the feet of contemptuous courtiers, had now become (as in Spenser's grim satire) the Lion who stalked, rampant and blood-stained into the Queen's private presence. As to the degree of intimacy between Elizabeth and Topcliffe, it was obviously less than he filthily boasted of, yet more than that between servant and employer. During the years 1593 and 1594 he had swollen to proportions of oriental nightmare:

> Mr Topcliffe caused Nicholas Jones to bring Atkinson unto him at ten of the clock at night, Mr Topcliffe lying in his bed, having his sword drawn lying thereupon. Jones, bringing in Atkinson, commanded him to kneel down at Mr Topcliffe's bedside, laying paper and ink before him, and commanding him to write what he could say, concerning priests resorting unto Mapledurham, my house. Whereunto he protested he could say nothing of any such matter. Then Nicholas Jones swore, that unless he told another tale he would dash out his brains with his sword; and Mr Topcliffe swore that, if he would not accuse me, he would chop off his legs with his sword that lay there; he would break his thighs, send him to a place where the plague would devour him (being, at that time, in the city of London), or else where the rats should eat the flesh from his bones. So as, through the threats of these two, he was compelled to set down whatsoever they two would have him to set down, or dictated unto him; which he did with such trembling that Jones asked him if he were troubled with a quaking ague.

Two nights later, Topcliffe copied Jones's witticism about the ague:

> The second night after, at ten of the clock, Jones brought Thompson to Mr Topcliffe's chamber, where he fell of such a trembling, that his teeth chattered in his head, and Mr Topcliffe asked him if he had an ague.

Jones was Topcliffe's familiar ("my boy Nicholas"), to whom he handed over Anne Bellamy after he had deflowered her and forced her to betray Southwell and her family. With her mother, a lady whose estate he was after, he used the same shock-tactics as with men:

> He beginneth with her mother, threatening her that, unless she would condescend to that which her daughter accused her of, he would pick out a jury out of Middlesex that should condemn her, he would hang her—reviling her, calling her old——, old witch, dishonesting her that . . .: so as, through his threatening, and hoping to escape, she set her hand unto whatsoever he has set down before. But, contrary to her hope, he committed her close prisoner to the Gatehouse, where she remained not the space of two hours but she declared all this unto Mrs Settle, a minister's wife, which was put unto her for company, who likewise justified this to Mr Topcliffe's face, in justice Young's house.

In another old lady, by contrast, his animal fury caused no fear at all, although he had had her sentenced to be pressed alive:

> Upon a time her friend Topcliffe passed under her window, being mounted upon a goodly horse going to the Queen, and Mrs Wiseman espying him thought it would not be amiss to wash him with a little holy water, therefore took some which she had by her, and flung it upon him and his horse, as he came under her window. It was a wonderful thing to see: no sooner had the holy water touched the horse, but presently it seems it could not endure its rider, for the horse began so to kick and fling that he never ceased till his master Topcliffe was flung to the ground, who looked up to the window and raged against Mrs Wiseman calling her an old witch, who, by her charms, had made his horse to lay him on the ground, but she with good reason laughed to see that holy water had given him so fine a fall.

If Topcliffe took this as an omen, he was right. By 1595, it became apparent that the policy of bludgeoning had failed. The Catholics stood firmer under it than under more subtle pressure. Topcliffe was defeated by the concentrated heroism of countless victims known and unknown, men like Swithin Wells who "being much urged (i.e. railed at) by Topcliffe at his death, prayed earnestly for him, desiring that God would make him of a Saul a Paul." When Topcliffe's mad raging met the tired contempt of men like Southwell and Gerard, it fizzled out in froth and splutter.

At Southwell's trial in 1595—

> Often they interrupted him, that he could seldom or never end one sentence, which he did begin.

70

Fr S.: I am decayed in memory with long and close imprisonment, and I have been tortured ten times. I had rather have endured ten executions. I speak not this for myself, but for others; that they may not be handled so inhumanly, to drive men to desperation, if it were possible.

Top.: If he were racked, let me die for it.

Fr S.: No: but it was as evil a torture, of late device.

Top.: I did but set him against a wall.

Fr S.: Thou art a bad man.

Top.: I would blow you all to dust if I could.

Fr S.: What, all?

Top.: Ay, all.

Fr S.: What, soul and body too?

(Upon the Attorney General intervening to explain Topcliffe's meaning) Topcliffe was very earnest and began to rail, but they would not permit him.

In the same year, Father Gerard was brought out, between bouts of torture, to write a confession. He wrote a denial of it.

While I was writing this, the old man waxed wroth. He shook with passion and would fain have snatched the paper from me.

"If you don't want me to write the truth" said I, "I'll not write at all." "Nay" quoth he, "write so and so, and I'll copy out what you have written." "I shall write what I please" I answered, "and not what you please. Show what I have written to the Council, for I shall add nothing but my name." Then I signed so near the writing that nothing could be put in between. The hot-tempered man, seeing himself disappointed, broke out into threats and blasphemies: "I'll get you into my power, and hang you in the air, and show you no mercy: and then I shall see what God will rescue you out of my hands."

The Cecils, father and son, were engaged at this period in delicate intrigues concerning the Succession. "Topcliffian methods" were becoming an embarrassment. The actual occasion of his downfall was typically Elizabethan. The Privy Council complained of his pecuniary profits. Lord Keeper Puckering solemnly questioned the legality of the Fitzherbert blood-money. Topcliffe answered rashly. Why should he not take a bribe of three thousand, when the Lord Keeper had taken one of ten thousand? There was a shocked silence. Even the Queen admitted that he had gone too far. A re-shuffling ensued that might have inspired Ben Jonson's *Sejanus*. The Lord of Misrule was committed to Westminster

Gaol. From there, his anguished whines penetrated to the Royal Ears:

> To your Majesty as to my goddess, I will explain, whensoever my service to come shall deserve that I may be admitted to your most joyful presence. . . . Since I was committed, wine in Westminster hath been given for joy of that news, and in all prisons rejoicings. It is like that the fresh dead bones of father Southwell at Tyburn and father Walpole at York, executed both since Shrovetide, will dance for joy. And now at Easter, instead of a Communion, many an Alelluia will be sung of priests and traitors in prisons and in ladies closets. . . .
>
> If it had not chanced as it did, I had been like to have taken a priest upon Palm Sunday at night. . . .
>
> To the God of Heaven and to yourself my Goddess on earth, I must say that my words and meaning was innocent and mistaken by his Lordship. . . .

The letter was dated "Good (or evil) Friday." On this same Good Friday he sent a gaoler to tell Fr Gerard: "he does not bear his imprisonment as patiently as I do mine." Love's Martyr! But hypocrisy is the tribute of vice to virtue. Did a faint flicker of decency trouble the soul of Topcliffe? If so, not for long. He came out of prison shortly after, and, in 1596, was let loose, with a rack, upon the gypsies of Northamptonshire.

In 1598 he made his last appearance against a Catholic, a Mr Barnes of Mapledurham, whose estate he coveted. Barnes was allowed free speech, and hit back with a crashing and meticulous indictment. He lost his liberty and risked his life ("for speaking against so good a statesman as Mr Topcliffe," said the Judge): but it worked. The public career of "Her Majesty's Servant" came to an end. Topcliffe, however, cannot be cited as another instance to Elizabeth's ingratitude to her faithful servants. She seems to have intervened on his behalf in his last blood-money dispute. With this salve to his sense of "injured merit," he retired to live the life of a country gentleman on the Fitzherbert estates.

In the year after the Queen's death, he was troubled by the hostility of his tenants, whom he accused of unmentionable vices, and by the efforts of Lord Shrewsbury to dislodge him from Padley. His last letter expresses his grief and bewilderment:

72

> That your Lordship whom God hath blessed with so many thousand pounds of stately lands . . . should now go about to offer to heave me (with your strength) out of Padley, a delightful solitary place, in which I took threefold the more pleasure for the nighness of it unto three of your chief usual houses, so there I thought that I should (in my old age) take comfort in your Lordship's presence.

He was still in precarious possession of Padley, when he died in 1604 at the age of seventy-two. The duration of his mortal life thus concided with, just overlapping, that of the great Queen whom he had so intimately and assidously served.

In the dream of life, devotion to Elizabeth was his elixir; it coincided with devotion to himself. In the awakening of death, it is likely to have been his undoing; it qualifies him for the Pain of Loss. With the Pain of Sense he had long had an unholy compact. But, then, so have many thugs and pugs whom only a Calvinist could imagine as damned eternally. Judas the Dreamer, not Barabbas the Brute, is the object-lesson. It would be cold and dubious comfort to think of Topcliffe in Hell; it is salutary and instructive to think of Hell in Topcliffe.

References to Topcliffe in MSS., State Papers, contemporary narratives, etc., have been printed in the following works:
1. *Catholic Record Society*, vol. v, *passim*.
2. *Dictionary of National Biography*: Topcliffe.
3. Tierney-Dodd, *Church History*, vol. iii, appendix xxxvii.
4. Camm, *Forgotten Shrines*, appendix C.
5. Jessop, *One Generation of a Norfolk House*, pp. 71, 79.
6. Hamilton, *St. Monica's Chronicle*, 1548–1606, p. 82.
7. Morris, *John Gerard*, *passim*.
8. Foley, *Records*, vol. i, pp. 350 sq.
9. Strype, *Annals*, vol. iv, p. 9.

The Earl and the Alchemist

INTRODUCTION

THE Earl is Ferdinando Stanley, Lord Strange, who succeeded his father as Earl of Derby on 25 September 1593. The Alchemist is not so easily nameable. He is the shadow of something that began creeping towards Ferdinando in 1591. Two years later it fell upon him in the mystery known as the Hesketh Plot. The Hesketh Plot is what I am going to write about. The bare facts are that a man called Richard Hesketh came to see Ferdinando on the day that he became Earl of Derby. Two months later Hesketh was hanged for high treason. In the following April Ferdinando, aged thirty-five, died of a violent sickness which some ascribed to poison and others to witchcraft.

Those are undisputed facts. The story about them, after some variations, reached Camden's *Annals* in the following form: Hesketh brought messages from the exiles, Cardinal Allen and Sir William Stanley, and the Jesuits. They invited Ferdinando to become King of England, and threatened him with death if he revealed their plan. He revealed it. So he died —cut off, apparently, by poison. That is the version generally accepted, for example by Cokayne's *Complete Peerage*.

Historians have not bothered to test it, or bothered much at all about the Hesketh Plot. Ferdinando's claim to the throne (he was in undisputed line through his mother from Henry VII) was soon a forgotten might-have-been; and his actual claim to rememberance has been a literary one. He was patron of the company that presented the first plays of William Shakespeare.

74

As a matter of fact, the two claims should not be divorced. Professor Tillyard has shown how likely it is that Shakespeare, right from the start of his History Cycle, had a broadly political aim: to stress the evils that result from a disputed Succession. But the years when he was writing Parts 2 and 3 of *Henry VI* (which are now accepted as his own work) were just the years, 1591-2, when he was under Lord Strange's patronage, and when Lord Strange was in danger from Succession intrigues. My purpose is not to comment on Shakespeare. But I believe that in one specific play, Part 2 of *Henry VI*, he provides a better background for the Hesketh Plot than the usual history-book façade.

In Hall's *Chronicles* he had, of course, a grand story pregnant with analogies between the situations of 1446 and 1592: defeat in France, discontent at home, and two rival factions regarding the Succession. The ill-starred campaign in Brittany, subject of much political recrimination and popular discontent, was drifting towards the disaster at Craon (May 1592) where Englishmen, as their general complained, "ran away infinitely." A new concept in popular discontent was "the mob" or *mobile vulgus*,[1] something that a faction-leader could use, as York is said to have used Jack Cade. There is a good deal of evidence like this from a news letter of August:

> There were never more malcontents of all sorts, gents as well as others, insomuch that they seem to be at that point that they care not what stir may happen, or who could attempt it, so they might mend their conditions and avenge their injuries (Verstegan, August 1592. *Stonyhurst MSS.*)

The rival factions were those of the Queen's Ministers, the Cecils, and the Queen's favourite, the young Earl of Essex. As early as 1589 Essex had established himself as the champion of King James and his right of succession to Elizabeth. The Cecils were obliged to groom some other candidate, if only as a stalking-horse. By 1592, either faction had its own rival organisation of spies and stooges.

There was nothing, however, in Hall or Holinshed to show Shakespeare how to make a clear-cut theatrical pattern out

[1] Watson, *Decacordon*, 1602.

75

of the situation in 1446. He achieved this by masking the Contention of York and Lancaster behind the rivalry of two foreground figures, Suffolk and Duke Humphrey, and behind the personal feud of York and Somerset springing from accusations of military incompetence. With the elimination of Humphrey, first, and then of Suffolk, and with the fading-out of Somerset, the stage is left clear for the main contention. It is possible that the situation in 1592 supplied him with this pattern. For it was the death of the fallen favourite Hatton, the sentencing to death of Sir John Perrot, and the decline in favour of Sir Walter Raleigh that set the political stage for the main rivalry between the Earl of Essex and Sir Robert Cecil.

A certain tang of bluff eccentricity in Shakespeare's Duke Humphrey, the Lord Protector, recalls the luckless Perrot, late Lord Deputy of Ireland. But the similarity is woven closer by a Shakespearian refinement of intrigue which owes nothing to Hall or Holinshed. Shakespeare depicts Humphrey as being pulled down by a temporary and iniquitous *combination* between York and his Lancastrian rivals. This is a Shakespearian invention. But it seems really to have happened in the case of Perrot. The Queen did not wish his condemnation. His enemy Hatton had died in disfavour. Both Cecil and Essex, who between them were all-powerful, knew that the charges against Perrot—that he had conspired with the King of Spain and Sir William Stanley—were the forged fabrications of a renegade priest. They could easily have discredited them. But they allowed their odium to pass unchallenged and to pre-judge the verdict.

The figure of the renegade double-crossing priest is introduced by Shakespeare into the scene where Humphrey's wife, Eleanor, is caught trying to determine the Succession by witchcraft. Shakespeare has transferred this scene, recorded by Hall under 1441, to the conspiracy against Humphrey in 1446. In the play, Eleanor is trapped, with York's assistance, by means of a priest who takes money from both sides. There is nothing about this in the *Chronicles*. It is a Tudor refinement introduced by Shakespeare. He could hardly have foreseen that another Royal lady, the Countess of Derby, Ferdinando's mother, was to be disgraced on exactly the same charge in 1595; but the use of sorcerers as *agents provocateurs* has been going on for some years before that.

These two devices—the combination of two deadly rivals to destroy a third party, and the use of sorcerers as *agents provocateurs*—happen to be those which are most essential to unlocking the Hesketh Mystery. It may or may not be that Shakespeare borrowed them from contemporary practice. If he did, it would add a spice of interest. But my inquiry is already a detective-problem in its own right.

It falls into two questions:

(1) Who was responsible for sending Hesketh to Ferdinando?

(2) Was there a connection between Hesketh's death and Ferdinando's?

These questions will occupy Parts II and III of the present study. Meanwhile, I will disentangle from their backgrounds the two principal figures: the glittering, high-bred, sensitive Ferdinando, Spenser's *Amyntas*, and the shadowy, nondescript form of Richard Hesketh.

I

God forbid any malice should prevail
That faultless may condemn a nobleman.
(2. *H.VI.* 3. ii)

In the land between the Pennine Range and the Dee and Ribble estuaries, the House of Stanley was the peak of a feudal edifice of families, Hesketh, Hoghton, Gerard, Langton, Shireburne, and many others, cemented by constant intermarriage. The Derby Household Books are full of their visits and feasts.[1]

One entry for Christmas 1587 is worth quoting: "On Saturday Sir Tho. Hesketh Players went awaie . . ."; for this was the Sir Thomas Hesketh of Rufford to whom Alexander Hoghton of Lea in his will of 1581 had commended his players and "Will Shakeshaft"—who was once supposed to

[1] Stanley Papers II, *Chetham Society, xxxi.*

77

be Shakespeare, and it may be that he was, and that thus he entered the Derby household.

Most of these families were Catholic, open or secret. The Hesketh of Rufford and of Poulton were open recusants; William of Poulton had married the sister of Dr Allen, the exiled Catholic leader, and his son was Allen's Secretary. But the Richard Hesketh of this study belonged to the Aughton branch that was predominantly Protestant. Here is the genealogy:

HESKETH of Rufford.

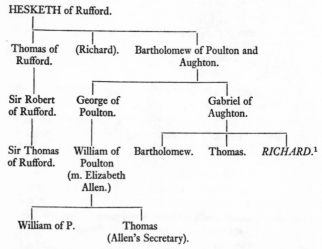

Of the three Aughton brothers, Batholomew was a "temporiser," but Thomas was a keen anti-Catholic lawyer, later Attorney to the Court of Wards, and Richard also, on his own evidence, was a decided Protestant. In 1581 he was a merchant, holding the half-commercial, half-diplomatic post of Agent at Antwerp. He was also a confidential friend and helper of the Queen's eccentric but influential favourite, Dr Dee, the astrologer and alchemist, whose *Diary* has the following, in the Latin used for its more portentous utterances:

Aug. 12th (1581). Through the deligence in my affairs of my friend Richard Hesketh, Agent at Antwerp, I received a letter from Dr

[1] The version in *D.N.B.* is wrong, as Sir E. K. Chambers has pointed out in his *Shakespearian Gleanings* (O.U.P., 1944), p. 55.

Andreas Hess, the student of occult philosophy, and along with the letter I received *Mercurii Mensitam seu Sigillam Planetarum.*

Hesketh's association with Dee is confirmed by a newswriter, Verstegan, long resident in Antwerp:

The man's name was Richard Hesketh, he had been sometime a merchant, but was fallen into decay by dealing with alchemists.

A few years later the positions were reversed. Hesketh had returned to his native Lancashire, while Dee and his "skryer" (or medium) Edward Kelley had migrated abroad to Prague, where the Emperor Rudolf's patronage proved more lucrative than Queen Elizabeth's had been. Dee was a sorcerer rather than a genuine alchemist. His search for the elixir of gold was incidental to his main passion, which was to descry the future and "call spirits from the vasty deep." Kelley, on the other hand, was a keen if fraudulent transmuter of metals; he had had his ears cropped for "coining" in Lancashire, but he acquired more skill under Dr Dee. As his skill grew, he became more and more independent of his master, until the great day came when his experiments succeeded and *gold* appeared in the crucible. Chaucer's world would have laughed or yawned, but the sixteenth-century potentates were all agog. Kelley became an international celebrity and a national asset. He was knighted by the Emperor Rudolf. From Lord Burghley in England there began to arrive a series of almost fulsome letters begging the "good knight" to return and offer the fruits of his genius to his Sovereign who was anxious to overlook any past misunderstandings. But Kelley, with no ear-tips left to tingle, was enjoying himself. Famous men like Edward Dyer, the poet and courtier, were completely under his spell year after year. It was Dyer who spread Kelley's fame in the English Court. He and others like him who had been devotees of Dee now deserted the master for the disciple. In the end it was Dee who came home in dejection in 1589 to the ransacked house at Mortlake.

On his return he renewed an acquaintance that must be carefully noted. Ten years earlier, a certain Richard Hickman, a *protégé* of Sir Christopher Hatton, had introduced to Dee his two nephews, Bartholomew and William Hickman. They appear to have been in confidential employment about the law courts; Lord Keeper Puckering may have taken them on when he succeeded Hatton. But on Dee's return Bartholomew Hickman began to act as his "skryer" in place of the absent Kelley. In the riot of names that confuses this study, the name of *Hickman* should be singled out and kept in a special compartment of the memory, not be confused with Hesketh.

Meanwhile in this same year, 1589, Hesketh had been forced to leave his home in Over Darwen and go abroad again. He had been one of the tenants of Thomas Langton, "Baron" of Newton, who held most of the land between Bolton and Blackburn, when an unfortunate affray occurred. Eighty of Langton's tenants set out to recover some cattle from the lands of Thomas Hoghton of Lea, and Hoghton was killed in the ensuing fracas. Walsingham, as Chancellor of the Duchy of Lancaster, took the matter very seriously. Langton and forty of his tenants were arrested and charged with murder. No jury in Lancashire could be found to try them. But Hesketh had not waited to be arrested and charged, perhaps because he was too near the actual slaying. He made for Prague, and joined the entourage of Sir Edward Kelley. During these years there were two types of Englishmen converging on Prague, with overlapping activities. There was a thin and furtive "gold-rush" of people like one Henry Leigh, steward of the Dacres estates, who "by the cause of my fortune was driven to go to Prague to seek some favour of Sir Edward Kelley." And there were agents like one Thomas Webbe, who was sent to keep an eye on the experiments of Kelley, and on Dyer, who was himself supposed to be keeping an eye on Kelley.

The Queen was still most anxious for Kelley's return. But, in April 1591, even as Lord Burghley was penning a last hortatory letter, disaster occurred. The emperor gave ear to Kelley's enemies, and the knight was hurled into prison. Dyer, too, was put under house arrest until a resounding Latin letter in Elizabeth's best style procured his release. The English gold-seekers, bereft of their patron, turned for protection elsewhere: to an English Jesuit in Prague named Father Thomas Stephenson. This man who afterwards worked for twenty years in England, has a reputation for integrity above reproach. No one has ever attempted to incriminate him in the alleged plot. He helped his fellow-countrymen out of sheer goodness of heart, though no doubt he hoped to convert them as well. Kelley's imprisonment was eased and he began to return to favour. Hesketh and Leigh found lodgings with a friend of Fr Stephenson, a fellow-Lancastrian, a goldsmith named Abraham Falcon. In the Falcon family-circle we have the first glimpse of Hesketh as a human being. It is not a sinister one. He appears as a jolly elderly fellow with a touch of the Lancashire comic. "Yellow-haired," he is described later, "a stout man, fifty years of age, clothed in yellow fustian with lace after the English manner."

It seems a far cry from the alchemists in Prague to Ferdinando, now Deputy-Lieutenant to his father in Lancashire and Cheshire. But it would be only too easy to trace a connection. Hesketh, Dee, and Dyer lead us straight to that occult circle of scholars, poets, and noblemen that has been christened "The School of Night." It is agreed that when Shakespeare flung out this phrase he was aiming at "Sir Walter Raleigh's School of Atheism," and also at a group of nobles praised as occult philosophers by Chapman in the dedication to his *Shadow of Night* (1594.) Now the first of this group is the Earl of Derby, "ingenious Darbie," who is praised also in the second hymn as "Ganymede." It is important to settle whether this occult philosopher, "ingenious Darbie," is Ferdinando.

Miss Bradbrook in her brilliant reconstruction, *The School of Night*, accepting the general opinion that he is, refers to him *en passant* as "an alchemist, and also suspected of witchcraft," as "a Catholic," and as "very unpopular." But I think the evidence shows that it was not he but his brother William, the Sixth Earl, who was the alchemist, and that Ferdinando was certainly not unpopular—*until* the Hesketh affair.

Until the Hesketh affair, Ferdinando and Essex were close friends, as may be seen, restropectively, in their letters (Lodge: *Illustrations*, ii.) But Essex was the declared enemy of all this occult business. Shakespeare's comedy *Love's Labour's Lost*, written probably in autumn 1593 at the request of the Essex

F   81

circle, is the story of four young friends who escape from the pseudo-mystical misogyny of the *Shadow of Night*; and of these four it seems obvious that "Ferdinand, King of Navarre" is a stately profile of Ferdinando, and "Berowne" is a quizzical compliment to the Earl of Essex. It seems more likely, then, that "ingenious Darbie" was not Ferdinando, but William, who became Derby on 16 April—especially since Chapman made last-minute revisions to suit political changes in 1594. It would be more likely still if the publishing date, 1594, went by the legal year which began on March 25th. But I am not sure about this.

In any case, it is clear that Ferdinando was happily married to a beautiful wife, their only sorrow being that they had no son but only daughters; whereas William was an intimate of Dr Dee, a recluse, and a "misogynist"—though later tied in most unhappy marriage to Burghley's granddaughter. There is much matter for reflection here. It is Ferdinando who emerges as the daylight figure shining and gracious, William as the bird of night. Yet it was William, evidently, who was Lord Burghley's candidate.

It is perhaps not accidental that Shakespeare invests Ferdinando with more dignity though less colour than "Berowne" (Essex). Ferdinando was a much older man, and he could already command in his own right the sort of feudal loyalty that Essex was trying by *condottiere* methods to amass. It is true that Ferdinando's followers were mostly Catholic; his bosom-friend Thomas Gerard, for instance, was brother to a famous and much-sought-after Jesuit. But he walked with great care in this regard. "Lord Strange gives good countenance to religion," says a report of 1590, "when he is with us." He had need to, for this same report had greatly alarmed Lord Burghley. "The number of recusants is great and doth daily increase," wrote the Bishop of Chester, complaining of "remiss execution of penalties." Burghley had a special map of Lancashire, one of Saxton's new ones, made for him; and put a cross against the names of many gentlemen whom he did not trust.[1] Through the new Chancellor of the Duchy, Sir Thomas Heneage, a devout Cecilian, means were also

---

[1] Cf. *Catholic Records*, vol. iv.

being sought of clipping the Stanley wings still further. One of Heneage's most aggressive instruments in this task was to be Thomas Hesketh, the brother of our Richard.

But there was nothing surprising in this attitude of suspicion, all candidates of the blood royal were under a sort of surveillance. It did not mean any enmity, such as existed between Essex and Sir Robert Cecil. With the soothing help of his wife Alice, who would sometimes add an effusive postscript to a rather cold letter, Ferdinando maintained good relations with the incalculable Sir Robert, who was now slipping quietly but irresistibly into his father's place. Nor is there any reason to doubt that Ferdinando enjoyed and loyally repaid, the trust and affection of Queen Elizabeth. While preferring the freedom of his native counties, he did his duties at Court with modest and pleasing success. He had taken part with Thomas Gerard among the thirteen pairs of knights in the famous tilting of 1590. And, in the Christmas festivities of the following year, his company of actors had a striking success, presenting six plays before the Queen as opposed to one each of the other companies. Altogether, in 1592 he stood at the full tide of his manhood—he was thirty-three—and of his wordly prospects. Yet, unknown to him, in May of the previous year the shadow had already fallen.

It is an event which demands the closest attention.

Locked away among Lord Burghley's papers was a document brought over by a secretly-renegade priest named John Cecil, who had been in Government employ at least since 1588. John Cecil is a person who would require a long chapter to himself; he was an adventurer of uncommon ability. But all that need be said here is that he and his còmpanion, another renegade named Fixer, came over with the intention of offering themselves as spies. On being taken before Sir Robert Cecil, they betrayed the new routes by which their fellow-priest were arriving, and the private letters entrusted to them by Catholic exiles; and then they produced a series of statements which may be read in the Domestic State Papers (238/160–3). There is some disagreement between one statement and another, but the main drift is that they were instructed *by Father Persons* to "seek entrance with my Lord

Strange and cause Catholics to cast their eyes upon him," and they were to keep their mission secret from all except from Fathers Garnet and Southwell. As an earnest of *bona fides*, they produced a letter purporting to come from Persons, instructing them to reply to him in the following terms:

> Your cousin the baker is well inclined and glad to hear of you, and meaneth not to give over his pretence to the old bakehouse you know of, but rather to put the same in suit when his ability shall serve.[1]

This they glossed as: "by baker and bakehouse is understood my Lord Strange and the title they would have him pretend when her Majesty dieth"—thus inculpating Ferdinando in some previous supposed negotiation. Sir Robert's only recorded reaction was a letter to his father of June 10 saying that John Cecil would do good work if he avoided the suspicions of his fellow-priests. Perhaps this attitude of off-hand approval reveals the true significance of John Cecil's information.

The written sources for Persons's life were once so difficult of access that historians have contented themselves, in sequence, with believing the worst. But in fact, while Persons's chief slanderers, Morgan and Paget and William Gifford, were hand-in-glove with would-be assassins and *agents provocateurs*, Parry, Savage, Ballard, George and Gilbert Gifford, this letter is the only factual evidence adduced against Persons of conspiracy in the proper sense of the word.

What sort of evidence is it? It is clean against Allen's and Persons's strict rule of *not* letting their seminary priests mix in politics, let alone such rash politics as this. It is clean against their consistent policy of *not* committing the Catholics to any definite English candidate. It is not in his own writing; it begins: "By reason of my indisposition . . . I cannot write this with my own hand," which is not an altogether encouraging sign of authenticity. It is against the trend of another letter of Persons of two months before which reveals quite casually that he has neglected to provide a channel of com-

---

[1] *Calendar of Hatfield MSS*. IV. 104. One may legitimately ask why this letter is not among the State Papers like the others brought over by John Cecil.

munication with John Cecil, and shows no anxiety to repair the neglect. In short, it is the production of John Cecil, whose subsequent record as a witness against Persons is notoriously unreliable.

But the point is that whether it was faked or genuine, whether Lord Burghley believed it or not, it was equally bad for Ferdinando. Consider what was happening that same year to Sir John Perrot, a great public servant and a sturdy Protestant. On the bare word of another renegade priest, the spy Denis O'Roghan, who received a life-pension of £40 for his services, on the strength of a letter that was "a manifest forgery" (*D.N.B.*), he was accused of conspiring with the King of Spain and Sir William Stanley; and after a year in the Tower, with his "memory impaired through grief and close confinement," he was sentenced to the traitor's death in June 1592.[1]

Nothing like that, of course, happened to Ferdinando. The John Cecil letter was never used in public. But it was kept. And in the spy-world, always eager for a new line of information, its muffled echoes appear to have spread. "All the Stanleys in England," the notorious Topcliffe is reported as saying in 1592, "are traitors."

In the Christmastide of 1591–2, when Ferdinando's players were presenting Shakespeare before the Queen, Allen was writing to Persons that John Cecil's treachery was now a certain fact. Had they really been guilty of the John Cecil letter, their only cue now was silence and extreme caution. But what happens in fact is that the espionage wires begin to hum with reports about Lord Strange and Sir William Stanley. "There is certainly intelligence between Strange and the Cardinal," wrote the spy Robinson (*vere* Barnes) to Phelippes from Brussels on June 13, 1592. In the following year, one William Goldsmith, having posed successfully as a Catholic in Rome "whereby I might have liberty to come amongst their wicked traitorous devotions," managed to procure some strictly non-commital letters of introduction from Cardinal Allen and his secretary to Sir William

[1] Cf. Tenison, *Elizabethan England*, IX. 84. He died with the sentence in suspense.

Stanley and to Dr Worthington, a Catholic divine in Brussels. Armed with these and with some gossip about Catholic hopes for Lord Strange, he hastened back to England, to Sir Robert Cecil, confident of a not unfriendly reception. In the same month, June 1593, the Portuguese spy Andrada, who lived on second-hand pickings, wrote to Burghley that Sir William Stanley was "determined to send into the kingdom a person of much understanding who can cause disturbance."[1]

This is the time and place, Brussels in the summer of 1593, in which Lord Burghley set his first version of the Hesketh Plot—a year after Hesketh's execution and six months after Ferdinando's death.[2]

On March 25th, runs Burghley's version, Hesketh was instructed by Stanley and Worthington to offer "a hallowed crown" to Lord Strange, and to incite him to rebel and depose the Queen. Between April and September, it continues, Hesketh wrote from Brussels to Rome and received directions and encouragement from Cardinal Allen. He then set out from Hamburg for England, and came to Lord Strange, then Earl of Derby, "*and persuaded him*," it concludes unequivocally, "*to undertake the same.*"

Passing over, for the present, Burghley's charge against Derby, and considering only that against Allen, we find the only known letter that Allen wrote to the Low Countries that summer was of a very different nature. It was known to Burghley, for it was intercepted, and he endorsed it. Its entitlement in Strype is:

> Cardinal Allen . . . upon report of a treaty between England and Spain to endeavour a liberty of religion for the Catholics. August 14, 1593.

It was intercepted because the peace offer made to Allen was not genuine; one of the messengers concerned in it was the

---

[1] *Calendar of Hatfield MSS.* IV. 330 and 335.
[2] Ibid. V. 58, 59. This, it should be noted, is not Camden's later story, but a quite different version, perhaps a rough draft, which was never published. The difference concerns Ferdinando's complicity. In *Sadler Papers*, III. 20, there is a very clever, ambiguous propaganda-version (date: about 1596) which may well be the intermediary between Burghley's first version which asserted Ferdinando's guilt, and Camden's later account which denied it.

notorious spy Robert Poley who had lately been present at the slaying of Christopher Marlowe.

A feigned peace offer to conceal a hostile thrust was an accepted political trick. But Allen was so anxious for this offer to be genuine that he half-believed it. To his correspondent, Richard Hopkins, an exile of high repute who had received the message, he wrote:

> Only we want good grounds of Her Majesty's intention and good acceptation of our travails therein; which if you can by writing or other equivalent means obtain, let me alone for the rest, promising mine own pains without exception, and not much doubting but that His Holiness will most favourably and earnestly employ his authority for the same.

In its entirety it is a noble letter. Indeed, no one who has studied Allen has ever doubted the pathos and sincerity of this, the last, year of his mortal life. He knew that a settlement would mean his own eclipse, for he had gone too far against the Queen, but he was eager to lay down his life for it, if it would mean true peace and freedom for his flock.

The natural impulse would be to reject decisively Burghley's accusation against him—made after his death, be it noted. But if one does that, the alternative seems so fantastic. The alternative is that Burghley himself, or someone near him, was the contriver of Hesketh's mission to England. One hesitates to accept this, if only from the less worthy fear of being thought a crank.

So perhaps the best thing will be not to jump to either conclusion—for this is a complex affair—but to follow Hesketh's movements in England. For it is certain that he did arrive in England in September, and it is equally certain that he arrived with a government permission or passport perfectly in order.

But as has been said—this is a complex affair.

II

'Tis dangerous when the baser nature comes
Between the pass and fell incenséd points
Of mighty opposites. (*Hamlet*, V. 2.)

Landing on September 9th at one of the Cinque Ports Hesketh made his way on foot to Canterbury. Although he had fled the country four years earlier to escape a murder charge, his behaviour was not that of a furtive outlaw. He did things in style. At *The Bell* in Canterbury he engaged a fellow-traveller, one Trumpeter Baylie discharged from the wars, to be his servant. Baylie was an honest lad, and Hesketh a kind master to him. His evidence about the next three weeks agrees reliably with that given by others.[1]

Their route lay from Canterbury through Rochester to Gravesend, and then up the river to London. Since Hesketh entered England freely, and was supplied with a passport, the presumption is that he got the actual document after landing, either from the Acting Secretary, Cecil, or from the Warden of the Ports, Lord Cobham (Cecil's father-in-law.) This presumption is justified by an important and intricate piece of evidence, which need be given here only so far as affects the present issue. It is this. Some weeks later, on 15th October, Hesketh wrote a letter addressed: "To Lord Cobham or Sir Robert Cecil," which began: "*I have hereinclosed sent your Honour the two letters I promised. . . .*" (*Ibid.*, p. 389.)

Now, these letters were then sent in a disguised manner by the Government to Hesketh's friends in Prague, Stephenson and Falcon. They replied immediately; and Stephenson's reply says: "I received your letter . . . dated the 20th of September, according to your count." So it follows that Hesketh promised these letters either to Cobham or to Cecil before the date of writing them, the 20th September.[2]

By that date he was well on his way to Lancashire. So, well before that date, he had had an interview, or some sort of communication, with Cobham or with Cecil. Of the two, Cobham is the more likely because Cecil was with the Court at Windsor in September (his interview with Hesketh came later), whereas Cobham was probably at his house, Cobham Hall, which

[1] *Cal. Hatf. MSS.* IV. 408. It is he who tells us about Hesketh's passport.

[2] "Promised" means "promised to write," not "promised to produce," because Hesketh was in close confinement by 15th October. It is possible, of course, that the date was faked for some reason, and that the letters were really written much later than September 20th and much nearer 15th October. If the reader prefers this interpretation, he must make the necessary adjustments. But he will note that either interpretation is equally fatal to the idea of Hesketh as a trusted agent of the Catholic exiles.

lay on Hesketh's route between Rochester and Gravesend.

On arriving in London the two spent a night at St Paul's Wharf; but they did not stay long in the capital. They were not seeing Elizabethan London at its best. Along with the worst plague in living memory there was a good deal of active discontent, as well as a profound unease about the nameless Succession. They spent another night at Hampstead. Then, on the morning of the 16th, as they were leaving *The White Lion* in Islington, something happened which seemed casual enough; but, on inspection, it turns out to be charged with the most urgent significance. *Hesketh was given a letter* "from one Mr Hickman" *to take to the Earl of Derby*.

Bang, for good, goes the idea of Hesketh as a secret agent—unless "Mr Hickman" was also in the plot. Here is how Hesketh described the incident to his interrogators, in terms too circumstantial to be doubted:

> A boy of the house named John Waterworth, in presence of the rest of the servants, as I remember, did deliver me a letter endorsed and directed to my late Lord of Derby, deceased, which they told me was from one Mr. Hickman, my lord's man, which letter, together with my passports, the next day after the death of my old lord were delivered to this lord at my request and for my discharge of the same letter (*Ibid.*, 409.)

"Mr Hickman, my lord's man"? It is not clear to us which lord. But it was clear, evidently, to the interrogators, Cecil and his law-officers; they did not afterwards inquire, "which lord?" It is also abundantly clear that Hickman had detailed knowledge of Hesketh; no inn-servant would have accepted this letter to an Earl without precise instructions. The scene is vivid: the boy coming forward at the last moment, the other servants watching. Hickman knew that Hesketh had returned after four years abroad, that he was due at Islington on the 16th, that he was going to Lancashire and would have to visit the Lord-Lieutenant to show his passport. In the absence of some other Hickman who knew both Hesketh and the law officers, it is a reasonable presumption that this was one of the Hickmans, already described in Part I, who were familiar with Dr Dee. Some entries in Dee's *Diary* confirm the presumption.

Chancellor Hatton, the Hickman's patron, had died in 1591 and been succeeded in the office by Sir John Puckering as Lord Keeper. In the August before Hesketh's arrival, Dee had been in exceptional demand by the Lord Keeper. He dined twice with him at Kew; and on a third occasion, 28 August, he recorded: "I was all day with the Lord Keeper. Mr Web and the philosopher came." The philosopher remains a question mark. But "Mr Web" was Thomas Webbe, the agent, who had returned from Prague.[1] The Hickmans, who also lived at Kew, were much about the place. A typical entry is: "September 20th. Barthilmew Hikman came to Mortlake." One may add another, for 23 March of the following year: "I gave Barthilmew Hikman the nag which the Lord Keeper had given me. Barthilmew Hikman and William his brother went homeward" (their home was in the Midlands.) Neither Hickman seems to have had a very high character. Dee later discovered that all Bartholomew's spiritualist prophecies were drivel and deceit. And, a month after Ferdinando's death, William Hickman offered Cecil £1,000 for the Receivership of Wards, with an extra hundred thrown in for Cecil's wife, but was refused.

It is too early, however, to follow up these suspicions. What is now certain is that Hesketh's reasons for visiting the Earl of Derby had been imposed on him by people who had nothing to do with the Catholic exiles. He had to present his passport (presumably signed by Cobham) to show that he was no longer wanted on the Hoghton murder charge; and he had to deliver this letter.

On the evidence of Baylie, he showed no undue anxiety to do either. Approaching Lancashire about the 20th, his first thought was for his wife and family; he did not turn east towards the Earl's house, but climbed on over the hard, high fell-country to Over Darwen. He joked about his wife in the letter to Falcon which he dated the 20th, and about his need to get back to her; so it is likely that he was a faithful husband.

[1] If Hesketh shipped at *Hamburg*, he probably came from Prague, not Brussels.

90

(His chief concern after his arrest was for her welfare.) She is described as "a painful housewife," with "many children." He spent the week-end resting with his wife; and then on Tuesday the 25th, he set out for Lathom, the Earl's Lancashire seat, still accompanied by Baylie, this time on horseback. But when they got there, the old Earl was no more; he had died that day. It was not the time to intrude. Hesketh pushed on to the house of his brother Bartholomew at Aughton, not far distant. His brother was away, but the household received him. Riding back to Lathom on Thursday he encountered Bartholomew and some friends returning, at Ormskirk; and they had converse together, but always in company. At Lathom he handed in Hickman's letter and his passport to Sir Edward Stanley, a Catholic relative of Derby's. His passport was examined by the new Earl, and by the Bishop of Chester who was staying at Lathom, and proved satisfactory.

Hesketh, having discharged his duties, was anxious to get back and spend Michaelmas with his wife and family. But Sir Edward Stanley detained him in conversation, in the course of which he told Hesketh that the letter he had brought was not important, it contained only the news of plague-deaths in London. It looks as if Stanley was sounding him as to what he knew of the letter; and it is clear that he accepted Stanley's story as the truth. Stanley then said that the Earl when he had more leisure would like to speak with him, and wished him to stay for a day or two at Lathom. Puzzled, flattered, and embarrassed, Hesketh accepted, and stayed there over Michaelmas, during which time he met his former landlord, Thomas Langton, the Baron of Newton, one of the new Earl's intimates (also a Catholic), and was friendlily entertained by him. The Earl saw him occasionally, but kept deferring any serious conversation. Finally, he said that he took so much pleasure in his company that Hesketh must go with him to Court; and he appointed a meeting-place for Tuesday, 2nd October, at "Brewerton" (or Brereton) in Cheshire. This was the seat of Sir William Brereton, a gentleman held in high repute in the county, though he is also named as a recusant.[1]

Hesketh, all unsuspecting, spent Monday night with his

[1] *Catholic Records*, VIII, 102.

brother at Aughton; and next morning he rode to Brereton (some forty miles south of Lathom) in company with Thomas Langton. That night he wrote two letters and despatched them by his servant, the Trumpeter, from whom he now parted. One was to poor Isabel his wife, the other to his other brother Thomas, the anti-Catholic lawyer. They are worth quoting in full, as showing his state of mind at that time. To Isabel he wrote:

> I commend me to you, desiring you to take in good part that I cannot come home again so speedily as I purposed, for that my lord that now is, having spoken with me somewhat at my first coming, did defer, by means of his sorrows and other business, the time from day to day; and having seen my passport hath taken such a liking of me that for his recreation I must needs keep him company to London or the Court, if by some good occasion I cannot rid myself. I have sent my man back whom I pray you receive and entreat well till my coming. I have partly left him with Mr. Baron [*i.e.* Langton] but to be at his choice to tarry or go to you. If he tarry with Mr. Baron, I have lent him the white nag, which he will use well, and no charges to you.
> From Brewerton, the 2nd of October.[1]

And to his brother:

> Having been so long out of the country, I was loth to come to you or any friend I had, before I saw how my Lord Lieutenant would accept of my coming, and the country think of me. It hath pleased my Lord that now is to request me to the Court with him for his recreation, which I cannot deny, but have granted. Brewerton, this 2nd of October, 1593.

On the 3rd, the cavalcade left Cheshire for the south. But the place and order of events are now not clear. All we know is that within the week Ferdinando had obtained an audience with the Queen at Windsor, and that Hesketh was under restraint in a house called "Sutton Park"; he was afterwards moved to Ditton Park, a house near Windsor.[2]

[1] *Cal. Hatf. MSS.*, IV, 381.
[2] England is full of Suttons; and the only clue to this one is that it was probably relatively remote from Windsor. It may be that the Earl confined Hesketh within his own jurisdiction of Cheshire, and then had him brought up later on and handed over: in which case "Sutton Park" might be Sutton House on the Cheshire border where Ferdinando's family once stayed on the way to London. Or it may be that he still had Hesketh in his retinue when he saw the Queen. In either case, after Hesketh fell into Government hands Ferdinando would be—and was—excluded from any share in the proceedings.

We do not know when or where, *or whether*, Ferdinando arrested him. It is highly probably that Ferdinando through his friends, Edward Stanley and Langton, had tested Hesketh shrewdly, and no longer doubted the man's personal *bona fides*. But he was thoroughly alarmed and put on his mettle by the thing that Hesketh had brought. It was to rid himself from the slime of some unknown aggressor, beyond Hesketh, that he rode to Windsor and went straight to see the Queen.

> Hence, thou suborned informer, a free soul
> When most impeached, stands least in thy controul.

The interview with the Queen was all he could have wished for. He left her presence, glowing with gratitude and relief. It seems certain that he showed her the Hickman letter, because, on her own initiative, she commanded Hesketh to be questioned about it. "Her Majesty is informed that you had a letter unto the Earl of Derby" (p. 409.) Had anyone else informed her, she would have suspected Ferdinando; and if she had suspected him, she would not have been content with Hesketh's answer. Hickman, at least, would have been called up and questioned.

Now, the really strange and sinister thing that we come up against is that, apart from this one question ordered by the Queen, and Hesketh's one answer to it, there is no other mention of Hickman or the Hickman letter in the whole affair. All sorts of other people who had had contacts with Hesketh—his brother, his servant, Thomas Langton, Henry Leigh—were called in and accused and questioned. But of Mr Hickman, whose letter was the only sure evidence of any communication between Hesketh and the Earl, there is no word. One can refuse of course to accept the argument *de silentio*; but the natural inference is that the Government wanted the Hickman letter hushed up, and that Hickman himself was employed by personages important enough to safeguard him from questioning.

Two other facts, already mentioned, must now be interpreted. The first is that Hesketh was given a passport, and, apparently, a pardon (a conditional pardon at least) for his flight from the murder charge of 1589. Such a pardon was

93

rarely given *gratis* to fugitives; they were promised it in return for some use to be made of them, either consciously as an agent or unconsciously as a dupe. Now Hesketh's behaviour was not that of a knowing agent. That is the second point: his artlessness. He simply had no idea that he was handling anything that might mortally endanger either the Earl or himself. He allowed himself to be led like a sheep to the slaughter.

It is important to bear in mind the comparative simplicity of Hesketh, for, in considering his reactions to captivity, one has to decide: whether he was a secret Catholic agent (though that is now almost out of the question), or a Government *agent-provocateur* (which might at first seem likely), or a dupe in a complicated scheme who had to suffer because the scheme had misfired.

The first thing that happened to him, *before* he was moved to a prison near Windsor, was a quick visit from Sir Robert Cecil.[1] This important interview is reflected in Hesketh's letter of the 15th, addressed "To Lord Cobham or Sir Robert Cecil," which must now be carefully considered. It has four paragraphs.

Its first two paragraphs rehearse confidential advice to Cecil as to how letters can be sent to Falcon and Stephenson in Prague in such a way that they will not suspect them of coming through Government channels. He is particularly anxious that "Mr Dear" (*i.e.*, Edward Dyer) should not learn of his arrest; otherwise he or his friends would write to Kelley's household in Prague, and then the Catholics would hear of it and suspect trickery. In the third paragraph he claims to have had conversations with Sir William Stanley and Doctor Worthington in Brussels, and to have left some notes of these conversations with his friends in Prague. These notes he now wishes to recover, "for the satisfaction of Your Honour [*i.e.* Cecil] on my behalf."

Here are problems whose final solution is buried in Hesketh's obscure past. Provisional answers must be contingent on the view one takes of his employment.

[1] The evidence for this is a note of Derby's of the 13th implying that Cecil had just returned from the visit, and a phrase in Hesketh's letter of the 15th: "in respect of what I told yr Honour the other day."

What sort of relations did he have with Stanley and Worthington in Brussels? He may, in the interval of his leaving Prague and coming to England, have sought employment with Stanley as a means of livelihood, or he may have done it under Government instructions, to pick up information. The latter is more likely because he does not confess it as a guilty secret; he avers it eagerly to clear himself from some other unspecified charge, "for the satisfaction of Your Honour on my behalf."

Why on earth should a record of conversations in Brussels be left in Prague? There is no clear answer to this on any interpretation of Hesketh's employment. There is nothing in any of his statements to show that these notes were connected with Ferdinando. But since he was writing for them at the behest of Cecil and Cobham, one can only suppose that they wished to establish some guilty connection between Prague and Brussels—perhaps between occult circles in Prague and Catholic exiles in Brussels.

Why should Dyer and his friends be so interested in Hesketh's movements that they would at once report news of his arrest to Kelley in Prague? This too must be left a mystery, but it may be that here we have a reason for Hesketh's guilty conscience which made him so eager to co-operate. The English Government was by this time highly suspicious of the alchemists in Prague. Dyer had come under a cloud that year; and Webbe the agent was about to be gaoled in December on the capital charge of "coining"—which caused Dr Dee "a flight of fear."

The fourth and last paragraph of the letter changes abruptly to a cry of terror. The reason is not far to seek. On 15 October, perhaps as he was actually penning his letter, his official cross-examiner arrived, William Wade, Clerk to the Privy Council. Wade slammed him right from the start with the blunt accusation, maintained right to the end: that he was not Hesketh the alchemist, but Hesketh the Cardinal's secretary come from Rome to stir up recusants in Lancashire. The poor man's letter ended with an appeal to Cecil to correct this error. But it is unlikely that he ever saw Cecil again. From now on till his execution he was in the expert hands of Wade.

The two sheets of his "confessions," dated November 4th

and 5th, one of which is badly mutilated,[1] obviously do not give the whole story. But they convey an outline. They are mainly piteous refutations of the wholly false charges that he was Allen's secretary and a stirrer-up of Lancashire recusants. He keeps repeating that he "was never reconciled" and has "no credit with recusants." He adds, with a touch of nobility, that he cannot tell lies against his neighbours to gain favour for himself. He alludes to "delivering my message to my Lord," and adds this:

> I would rather have lain in prison during my life, or suffered death, than I would have done this message for any Stranger's behoof.

This shows that he was not confessing a message from Catholic exiles, but another sort of message to the Earl which he had supposed to be innocent. This can only be the Hickman letter.

But as soon as he began to suspect the Hickman letter to be the cause of his misfortune, the written questions and answers ceased. The last knowledge we have of him is from a letter of Wade to Cecil of November the 29th, the day of his execution at St Alban's.

> I was at the arraignment of Hesketh, as I was commanded by my lord Keeper, but the man did confess the indictment and acknowledge all his former confessions and declarations to be true, so that there needed no other testimony against him (*Ibid.*, IV, 423.)

Evidently there had been some recantation of his voluntary statements to Sir Robert Cecil. He was trapped in the position familiar to stool-pigeons of the period, of having made declarations in the service of the Government and of then seeing the Government make use of those very declarations to break his neck. In the later propaganda story, he—

> bitterly with tears bewailed their acquaintance, and naming Sir William Stanley and others, cursed the time he had ever known any of them.[2]

No doubt the wails and curses included piteous denials and explanations. But when they had died away exhausted, it was

---

[1] This one is in the supplement to the Hatfield Calendar, XIII, 493.
[2] *Sadler Papers.* III. 20.

Wade's task to convince him that a simple avowal of "all his former confessions" was the wisest course. A man might plead guilty for several motives: fear of torture, hope of a last-minute pardon, promise of favour for wife and family. All or any of these motives may have led Hesketh to mumble assent to the indictment, "so that there needed no other testimony against him."

Nevertheless [continues Wade], Mr. Attorney-General laid open all the plot and course of his treasons for satisfaction of the standers-by, in very discreet sort, and did make collections out of his confessions. . . .

"Collections," and "very discreet" ones, were certainly necessary. For the Attorney-General, Sir Thomas Egerton, had to avoid any impression that Hesketh had come over with a Government passport, that he had had a letter planted on him in London, and that there was no evidence at all of any treasonable converse with the Earl or anyone else in England. The only evidence there could have been would have been that of the Earl himself. But Ferdinando was kept out of the proceedings, as will be seen later, by an omission that cast grave doubts on his loyalty. Failing this evidence, the man could presumably have been arraigned on, his earlier statements to Cecil, for "consorting with traitors overseas." But it seems clear that all they wanted of him was an admission that would enable them to proceed at once to the sentence without trial.

Wade's letter continues:

My lord Chief Justice, before the pronouncing of the Judgement, did use a very grave speech to the comfort of her Majesty's good subjects by these and the like graces God had shewed.

This high strain is then broken by a homely interpolation, somewhat in the nature of a belch:

I would have waited on you to have made relation thereof, but am troubled with so vehement and grievous indisposition in my stomach.

Wade's stomach-trouble was probably not the effect of the performance he had just witnessed, but of his strenuous rehearsals to make it a success. With unconscious irony he ended by telling Cecil of word from Nuremberg that

Hesketh's letter was well on its way to Prague—"by which you may perceive that there is discreet means and diligence used to recover the instructions he had of Worthington." This was the letter Hesketh had written to his friends in Prague, "for the satisfaction of your Honour on my behalf." It arrived in Prague the day before his execution.

A missive purporting to be "the instructions he had of Worthington" was found among Lord Burghley's papers when the archives were opened. But its contents, and his secrecy about it, are enough to stamp it as a forgery.[1] Over a thousand words long, couched rather in the style of Polonius to Reynaldo ("... and thereupon here pause, and see whether he will encourage you to speak out or not"), and quite alien to current Catholic policy, it is not the sort of "secret instruction" any sane man would risk falling into hostile hands. Nor did Lord Burghley, being a sane man, do so. Challenged by the Viceroy of the Netherlands to produce evidence for his vague accusations of encouraging Catholic plotters, he did not produce this. Probably, like the other draft accusing Ferdinando of conspiracy, it was an effort to provide evidence; but he very wisely decided it was not a successful effort. It seems best to respect his silence.

But long before any possibility of acknowledging or denying it, the gallows were up for Hesketh. On November 28th—December the 8th and the Feast of Our Lady's Conception, by the new style of Catholic Christendom—while he waited in his cell, Falcon and Stephenson were writing him warm-hearted replies, and his homecoming was being toasted by Falcon's family "in a pot of bitter beer." It might have comforted Hesketh strangely to know that. For, apart from his

[1] Falcon in his reply to Hesketh (IV. 336, misdated) speaks of a sealed packet which he has found according to Hesketh's instructions and is forwarding. He also speaks of a pleasant gentleman called Mr Samuel Lewkenor who had just arrived, is lodged in Hesketh's rooms, and is sending back a letter of his own along with Falcon's. This Mr Lewkenor who imposed so easily on Falcon was an agent of Cecil's, to whom he returned shortly (IV. 603). It is an obvious guess that he put the sealed packet where Hesketh (writing while he still hoped for a pardon) told Falcon it would be. But the missive purporting to be "the instructions" is dubious enough without adding this conjecture. Seals could be, and were, expertly forged in London.

wife, for whose sake perhaps he had pleaded guilty, there was no one in England who cared a straw about him. As he waited to be dragged next morning on a hurdle to the gallows, he had none of the comfort of dying in a holy cause, nor even of a great crime cleansingly repented, but only the reproach of his own pusillanimity, and the scorn of omnipotent injustice. Still, the story (in *D.N.B.*) that he cursed and wailed *on the scaffold* is a mistaken addition. Fr Stephenson's letter ended: "Farewell, good, loving, and beloved Mr Hesketh, this present 8th of December. ..." It may be that the prayers of a good man reached him in a flash of time, and brought with them a memory of warm affection and an echo of the vesper bell from the great Church of the Virgin at Prague. He was certainly more sinned against than sinning.

The conclusion would seem to be that he was a carefully-chosen dupe. A guilty man on other grounds, he was simple and ignorant of political tensions in England, but he had connections both with occult circles in Prague and with Catholic exiles. He was sent into Lancashire with a passport which obliged him to visit the Earl of Derby; and on the way a letter was planted on him, addressed to the old Earl. If we are right that Mr Hickman was one of the Hickmans acquainted with the secrets of Doctor Dee, we can make a guess as to its contents.

It would be a cryptically-phrased astrological prediction (purporting to come from Prague) about the old order being eclipsed by the new, which might be construed either as "the bond cracked betwixt son and father," or as the rise of the House of Stanley over the House of Tudor, with a reference to the coming year of the Queen's climacteric.

The authors of the letter counted on it being handed to the *old* Earl, who was a stern but timorous man. The letter would have thrown him into a mixture of the terrible plights of Gloucester in *King Lear*, I. ii, and York in *Richard the Second*, V. iii. He would be led to suspect his son, perhaps of designs against himself, certainly of designs against the throne.

He would do one of two things. Either he would take the letter to Lord Burghley, that wise counsellor, and appeal to his mercy and discretion—in which case there would be consultations between the two old men, the production of fresh evidence (the John Cecil letter), and an agreement that the young man must be brought to heel, given a salutary fright, etc. Or, he would trust his son, destroy the letter, and do no more about it. In that case, sooner or later, some important personage would address him in some such words as these:

"One of your servants has laid a charge that one Heskit did bring you a *schema* astronomical. And the same has been talked of in London. You would have done more wisely to declare this business. You say you questioned Heskit and found him innocent of foreknowledge? But there is a paper which has now come to hand, which shows this Heskit to be an instrument of Cardinal Allen and Sir William Stanley. I fear that is not all. There was a letter two years past, which I had forgotten, but am now reminded of. It was a message to my lord your son—*from Parsons the Jesuit*."[1]

Beyond a doubt, the old Earl would have been scared rigid. From that time on, the heir of the house of Stanley would have been as wax under the Cecilian thumb—as indeed the unfortunate Earl William seems to have been, not to mention James I.

But, in the event, the authors of the letter had to deal unexpectedly with the new Earl, Ferdinando, whose portrait, if it shows anything, shows imagination, intellect, and decision. Ferdinando did the boldest and the safest thing. By holding Hesketh *incommunicado*, and then going straight to the Queen and winning her approval, he threw the fatal engine bouncing back towards the enemy.

But what we now have to consider is how he lost this great initial advantage, and became aware that the forces against him were stronger than he could fight.

III

Crooked eclipses 'gainst his glory fight (Sonnet 60).

If my reading of the situation is correct, Ferdinando's initial advantage with the Queen was counteracted by Sir Robert Cecil's interview with Hesketh. Cecil was able to

[1] For the John Cecil letter about Persons, cf. Part I.

return to the Queen with the sort of evidence that would inflame her imagination, and obscure the real origin of the Hickman letter. It was evidence of a seeming conjunction, in the person of Hesketh, between papist plotters in Brussels and occult astrologers in Prague.[1] Cecil took pains to foster this conjunction of occultism with papistry. Topcliffe's attempt to kill Mr Basset with a witchcraft charge—which led in 1595 to that strange case in English history, when Topcliffe sued in open court for breach of contract to pay for murder—was even then in progress. But Cecil's methods were less sensational than his henchman's. In October, he personally engaged the disreputable *agent provocateur*, Benjamin Beard, to get to work on a certain Mrs Shelley, a fallen Catholic "who hath gone about to sorcerers, witches, and charmers, to know the time of Your Majesty's death, and what shall become of the State" (*Ibid.*, p. 402.)

How can one help being suspicious when one finds, a year or so later, that Ferdinando's mother, Henry VII's descendant, had fallen into disgrace on exactly the same charge? It was so notoriously a capital offence[2] and so feared and detested by the Queen. There is precedent for suggesting that the charge was framed against the mother (and then dropped) in order to stop her disputing the same charge made against her son.

Meanwhile, after a visit to his mother, who lived in the south (long estranged from the old Earl), Ferdinando returned to Lancashire, early in November. Although he was the only possible witness against Hesketh, Cecil and his close circle of law-officers excluded him from any share in the proceedings. The fact, and presumably the reason, was that he was really a witness in Hesketh's favour, since the only tangible evidence of Hesketh's communication with him was the Hickman letter. It seems that only after his return did he become aware that Sir William Stanley was supposedly involved in the case. Alarmed by malicious rumours, because Stanley's two sons were among his personal retainers, he wrote to Cecil on the

[1] A protest to the Emperor about Kelley seems to have been initiated about this time, and then dropped later in November. *Hatfield Calendar*, IV, p. 417.
[2] By the Statute of 1581 (23. Eliz. c. 2). Ewen, *Witch-Hunting and Witch-Trials*, p. 18.

7th, asking whether it was the Queen's pleasure he should keep the young men still about him. Both he and his wife were now sure that there was a plot against him in high places; but Alice was all for keeping in with Cecil at whatever cost. The next paragraph, however, shows that the Queen was still upholding him.

On Thursday the 20th, Puckering wrote to Cecil that the indictment against Hesketh was complete; it only remained for him to wait on the Queen "to know her pleasure in such points as, in the mean, may be found meet to inform her Highness." But the Queen's idea of what was meet differed from Puckering's. Over the weekend, he wrote again to Cecil, this time in some perplexity:

> Her Majesty is pleased that it be opened in the evidence against Hesketh that my lord of Derby, being by him moved, etc., did presently apprehend the party, and made it known to Her Majesty. Mr. Attorney herein desireth to be advertised from you or some other that knoweth this to be so, that he may have some warrant of that he shall affirm therein, having otherwise no ground as of himself, either of his own knowledge or by examination, to affirm it. (*Ibid.*, p. 421.)

So the Queen had to intervene personally to rescue Ferdinando's part in the affair from darkness and suspicion. There had been nothing at all in the indictment about his part in detecting the supposed treason. The cause of this omission, as the Attorney-General Egerton admitted, was that this vital evidence, which incidentally told almost as much in favour of Hesketh as of Ferdinando, was suppressed in the material supplied for the indictment by Cecil and Wade. This suppression is the key to the curious way in which Wade skirted the same evidence in his cross-examination of Hesketh. It also sheds a most ominous glare on the version of the plot drafted for Lord Burghley at the end of 1594: that is, at a time when both Hesketh and Ferdinando were dead:

> Hesketh . . . related to the said Lord Strange, then Earl of Derby, all the treasons and purposes aforesaid, and persuaded him to undertake the same.

Yet in his lifetime Ferdinando was never brought face to face with this cruel charge which the Treasurer was ready to propagate after his death.

As a prelude to the underground attack on him, Ferdinando found, on his return to Lancashire, that the malicious rumours were being circulated against him by none other than *Thomas* Hesketh, Richard's brother. He soon realised that the malice was much more than a family grudge. Thomas Hesketh was one of a group of lawyers whose task was to extend the powers of the Chancellor of the Duchy, Heneage, against the Lord Lieutenant. Others of the group were Beeston and Wilbraham, Receiver and Feodary of Cheshire and Sergeant Warburton. But, as Heneage wrote to Cecil: "None hath furthered Her Majesty's service in that country so much as Mr. Hesketh."

The struggle hinged decisively round the office of Chamberlain of Chester. Chester was a County Palatine; and the Chamberlain was "the mediate officer to all her Highnesse's superior courts of justice so as all writs and processes . . . are directed to the Chamberlain of Chester." Hitherto the office had been vested by hereditary right in the Earls of Derby. Even before his father's death, Ferdinando had sought to be jointly vested with him—and reasonably, since he discharged so many of his father's responsibilities as Lord Lieutenant.[1] Immediately after his father's death, he wrote to Cecil again, more urgently. He wrote a third time, on 20 October, in the first glow of confidence after his interview with the Queen; from his letter it looks as if she had verbally promised it to him.

But November wore on without an answer. Instead there came a reply from Chancellor Heneage to Cecil about Ferdinando's complaint against Thomas Hesketh. Heneage declined to consider it, and eulogised Thomas Hesketh exceedingly.

Meanwhile, Ferdinando had experienced a very unpleasant set-back in Lancashire. A warrant arrived for the arrest of his friend Thomas Langton, Baron of Newton, as an accomplice of Richard Hesketh. Langton was a county magnate of high standing (he was made Knight of the Bath by James I); and this insult was too much for Ferdinando who knew it to be false. He wrote very coldly to Cecil saying that he had already

[1] Earl William in his lifetime, 1625, did this for his son James.

103

satisfied himself as to the loyalty and innocence of the Baron of Newton. But the charges, framed by Wade, went forward: that Langton was a recusant (though this was not strictly true), and that: "Hesketh was directed to him. He knowing Hesketh to be come from overseas . . . brought him to the speech of the earl" (a palpable lie.)

In the arrest of Langton, Ferdinando had a glimpse of the ugly framework beneath Cecil's smooth veneer. The Countess Alice tried once more the effect of feminine appeal. Her letter betrays urgency:

> I doubt not but my lord shall be crossed in Court and crossed in his country, but I imagine his uprightness and honourable carriage will, by means of so good friends as your father and yourself, on whose love and kindness he chiefly and only doth rely, be able to support him against any malice, and to this let me be a mover.—A Derby. (*Ibid.*, p. 427.)

"Crossed in Court and crossed in his country." Her phrase was prophetically accurate. On 15 December he made a last desperate appeal for the Chamberlainship; it was vital to him, both for protection against machinations within his county, and as a sign of the Queen's confidence. But on the 27th, Burghley, benign as ever, decided that the office was "of a more large and absolute authority than is meet for a subject." Egerton provided him with precedents for giving it "to men of much meaner sort"; and a day or two later he gave it, unofficially, to Egerton.[1] There is no sign that the Queen approved, till months later.

The remote sequel is instructive. When James I succeeded, Egerton applied at once for renewal of the office; but James refused politely, and restored it to Earl William "whose ancestors long enjoyed the office." Clearly, its removal from Ferdinando in 1593 was equivalent to a public disgrace. When Christmas came, he did not go to Court.

The close of the year was for him a sad contrast with the

---

[1] *Egerton Papers* 192. Egerton, a bastard, and formerly a recusant and dependant of the Stanleys, seems almost to have stepped into Ferdinando's skin. He got his Chamberlainship, his private papers, his books, his manor of Brackley, his unfortunate widow (who seems to have had no choice), and the wardship of his daughters—the eldest of whom was a favourite for the Crown in 1600. All this without any personal rancour; he was simply serving Cecil to check every path to the Succession.

gay, triumphant Christmas of 1591. Sad and inexplicable: he had always kept clear of factions and policies. When he became Earl of Derby and received, shortly after, a singular token of the Queen's approval, his stature was among the highest in the kingdom. But that very week, the week of the Hesketh affair, marked the outset of a plunging decline.

A new step in the decline was his estrangement from the Earl of Essex. Hitherto they had been friends—like *Antonio* and *Bassanio*, Professor Dover Wilson had suggested. But early in December, when Essex was enjoying special favours from the Queen at Hampton Court, he wrote Ferdinando a languid letter of mingled complaint and mockery. It appears that some persons who had deserted Ferdinando's service for that of Essex had been found hanging around Lathom, perhaps to spy on him, and Ferdinando had had them ordered off. Essex then requested that if Fernando had a grievance against them, it should be settled before some magistrates. There is more in this than meets the eye; and it cannot have been meant except as a taunt, for to it was subjoined the remark that if Ferdinando had not broken their friendship, he would have got his Chamberlaincy of Chester by Essex's favour, and would thus have been spared these daily setbacks in his own county.[1]

Essex had great and endearing qualities. But in spite of his lineage, he lacked breeding. Ferdinando touched the point with a needle when he replied, in a fine letter of 19 December, that friendship between equals was not maintained by patronage, still less by threats. He left it to Essex to choose between the flattery of base and unnatural curs who having deserted one master would as likely desert another, and the true friendship of himself "whose love may ten times more steed you than such under-grooms' service." Essex replied, 17 January, that servants were free to change their masters; "but I see they are not to be reconciled to your favour, and you will be, as you say, righted by yourself; therefore I will leave you to your own way." It is clear from the exchange that these faithless retainers were at least partly responsible for Ferdinando's troubles "which fall out every day in this country."

[1] Lodge, *Illustrations*, ii, pp. 447–51.

One could build up a case that Essex was the real cause of Ferdinando's downfall; that his agents had contacted Hesketh in Flanders; but it would not surmount the stumbling-block of the Hickman letter. Perhaps the part played by Essex is best illustrated by the other plots that preceded and followed the Hesketh affair.

In the overthrow of Perrot, Cecil was the prime agent, and Essex, perhaps reluctantly, complied. In the Lopez plot (early 1594), it was Essex who struck, to foment the war with Spain; and the Cecils, inclined to peace, had grudgingly to follow. In the Yorke-Williams plot (late 1594) they both clashed again, but it is not certain which side moved first; Yorke came over with a passport from Essex, but Cecil's agents, Poley and Moody, had been busy for some time before.[1]

The Hesketh plot appears to be a case of the Cecils again striking first and Essex complying—but not so reluctantly, because Ferdinando was a bar to his dynastic ambitions. For Ferdinando the quarrel was an illustration of Robert Southwell's remark in his *Humble Supplication*: "Everyone trampleth upon their ruin whom a Prince's disgrace hath once overthrown." It was a lesson for Shakespeare, too.

In the new year, Ferdinando continued to be "crossed in his country." Thomas Hesketh was chiefly serving the Government through the Court of Wards, of which he was later to be Attorney. The Court of Wards was the most powerful weapon of the Cecils for distributing favour or displeasure. The Government policy especially in Catholic Lancashire, was to break up the family. In the case of Brereton of Handforth, Ferdinando tried to keep the child near his mother (Katherine Hurleston.) In the Lent term the case became a trial of strength between London pressure and local feeling; and—to anticipate a little—a triumphant letter from Wilbraham to Cecil reported how the Earl had been outfaced, and a verdict secured—

which would have been taken in very evil part against the Sergeant and us all by my Lord of Derby, if he had lived, as was manifested by the report of those that were very near to him.

[1] In the other plots of 1594, those of Cullen and Daniel, Cullen was a genuine fanatic bent on killing Antonio Perez and Daniel was a creature of Lord Burghley's.

"If he had lived . . ."?

The phrase has a sinister ring, uttered in those quarters which pressed on him with such mounting hostility. As early as December and January, rumours were current of forcible measures intended against the Earl. They reach us through Catholic channels, but they were not Catholic in origin; and the Catholic writers are careful to grade their reliability. One such is Richard Verstegan, whose intelligence from England was of a high quality. His own books and poems were widely read there.

His letter shows the Catholics as in the dark about the whole affair. He quotes as hearsay: that Hesketh had been in Stanley's regiment, that he was supposed to be the Cardinal's secretary; and corrects the latter from his own knowledge (confirmed, as we have seen, by Dee's *Diary*) that Hesketh was a Protestant merchant who practised alchemy. He then adds this important sentence: "But whether he were by the Earl of Derby detected or not is uncertain; for some report that the Earl is deprived of his liberty." An exaggeration, doubtless; but it could not have arisen without some ground for it.[1]

More clear-cut and significant is a letter to Cardinal Allen of 25 December, from his intimate friend Richard Hopkins, an elderly and distinguished exile whom we have met once already. Like Verstegan, he was an author of high repute; his popular translation of Luis de Granada was very widely read by both Protestants and Catholics; he had sent a copy of it to Sir Francis Walsingham on the grounds that all good religious men should value the pursuit of holiness. He possessed considerable critical acumen as well as a tolerant understanding of others.[2]

At the end of a long letter about other things, he devotes the last paragraph to a report, evidently a non-Catholic one, that has just come out of England—

> declaring in these words: "that one Hesketh was there executed for coming with a crown blessed by Doctor Allen and sent by Sir William

[1] There is also interesting evidence in the *Conference on the Next Succession*; but the true purpose and nature of this book is so little known and widely misrepresented that I must omit it here.

[2] I owe this information to Southern, *Elizabethan Recusant Prose*, pp. 196–206.

Stanley, by this Hesketh, to the Earl of Derby that now is; and that the Earl was in trouble about this matter."

Hopkins dismisses the "blessed crown" story as an old canard that was first raised twenty years ago; and then he adds his own opinion:

It seemeth that they are afraid of this Earl of Derby, and do devise this rumour to colour the apprehension and destruction of him.[1]

Hopkin's opinion has the value—no more and no less—of his own reputation for integrity, experience, and good sense. It sums up exactly the impression that we have already received from Cecil's papers.

But is this all too melodramatic? It is true I have found Shakespeare—from *Henry VI* to *Hamlet*—a better mirror of the age than the average text-book. But it is also true that the last twelve years of Elizabeth I's reign were full of dark and gruesome things; and historians have tended to shirk them. They were years of incessant internecine intrigue. The great imposthume that burst in 1600, when James threatened to cross the border with an army in support of Essex, had been gathering for ten years. By 1593 it was clear that England, by a conspiracy of silence, was being deprived of one chief benefit of monarchy: the prospect of a stable succession; the result was nerve-racking tension between all parties. There was no certainty, no probability even that the Queen would long outlive 1596. The crisis might blow up at very short notice. It was absolutely essential for the party in power, the Cecils, to keep a check on every possible path to the Succession.

Now it was well known that, by the terms of Henry VIII's will, the Dowager Countess of Derby and her two sons were the only unquestioned legitimate English heirs to the throne. On the other side, as has been said—but it needs stressing again—the obvious non-English heir, James of Scotland, was bound by links of intrigue to the Earl of Essex. The Cecils simply could not afford to let the Stanleys slip out of their control. Events show that they did not; the Dowager was silenced; Cecil's niece was married to William; Egerton got

[1] Cottonian MSS. Titus B., ii.f, 224.

the wardship of Ferdinando's daughters, and presided, as Lord Keeper, over the law-suits that kept William well subdued. But all that could only happen after Ferdinando's death. Meanwhile, in the path stood Ferdinando: very aloof, very cautious, not giving anything away.

Supposing you had a mind like Cecil's, confronted with a man like Ferdinando, what would you do to bring him to heel? You cannot sift him openly, for—out of loyalty or malice—he may expose you. Yet sift him you must. Your only chance is to approach him by indirections and anonymously, in a way that can never be proved against you, and get a hold over him by something very like blackmail. I believe I have made out a good case that that is, more or less precisely, what happened.

But when Ferdinando went straight to the Queen, the original scheme misfired and the engineers themselves, for a moment were almost hoist by it. He now ceased to be a neutral figure; and struggling still for independence, he became a menace. As a political factor, he had to be eliminated. And if the rest is surmise "whose murder yet is but fantastical," it may be well to remember that the Overbury murder would never have come to light, if the party in power had not wished it so.

After Ferdinando's death, the drift of surmise hardened into at least one concrete accusation. It comes to us through a woman, the Countess of Shrewsbury, Bess of Hardwicke's daughter, who, incidentally, played a part in detecting the Overbury murder. The Shrewsburys, guardians to Arabella, were vitally interested in the fate of Ferdinando; it is in their papers that are preserved his correspondence with Essex, and the post-mortem reports of the doctors and the Commissions. The present evidence is an account of a conversation of hers with her bailiff, and it can be dated between April and August, 1594.

In August, her bailiff, one Nicholas Williamson, deserted her service in the hope of entering that of Essex. He was arrested a year later and thoroughly sifted by Cecil. One might suspect the evidence of such a person; yet it has an undoubtedly authentic ring about it.[1] We are, for a moment,

---

[1] He protests he does not see the use of these reports, for his own self-defence is not believed, and the Countess has only to deny them, and he will be outfaced. *Cal. Hatf.*, *MSS.*, V., p. 253.

in a strange, exciting alcove, where snatches reach us of what people were actually saying and thinking:

"By God," said the Countess, "*My* lord at his coming to London shall go forth to dinner but to few places, and shall be provided against such practices."

The Countess named a definite poisoner. But Williamson, when it came to the point, shrank understandably from repeating the name to Cecil.

> My lady also one day told me of the manner and forcible death of my late lord of Derby, saying that some were of the opinion that my lord that now is, his brother, had procured him to be poisoned; "but," saith she, "I believe it not. But those foolish speeches that he spake to Mr. Francis Hastings, saying that they two should one day fight for the crown, the show of his great will and haughty stomach, his making of himself so popular and bearing himself so against my lord of Essex, I thought would be his overthrow."

Eventually, with much circumlocution, he admitted that she had named as the poisoner, a party that was connected with the party that opposed her husband in a notorious Star Chamber case. The party that opposed her husband were the Stanhopes. They were firm adherents of the Cecils.

As evidence of *murder* this is valueless. But it is good evidence that the Cecils had so *harried* Ferdinando that, when he did die a sudden and mysterious death, the conclusion seemed obvious. And certainly, his sickness was very strange and violent in an active man of thirty-five. He was taken ill after hunting on Friday in Easter Week, 5 April, and on the next day began to vomit blood and fleshy matter. This terrible vomiting continued for eight days in spite of all the physicians could do. He died in a corrupt and wasted condition on 16 April.

A post-mortem Commission was set up immediately under the direction of Egerton, the ever-ready, and Sir George Carey, Alice's brother-in-law—and, incidentally, a member of "the school of night." Egerton's recommendations were "not to prejudice the cause" by sticking to one particular line of inquiry, but to keep an open mind for any suggestion that might arise. A consequence of these recommendations may be seen in Carey's report to Cecil a week later that he had found "greater presumptions that the Earl of Derby was bewitched than poisoned."

But before the inquiry was directed to witchcraft, Carey let fall one "vehement suspicion"; it concerned Michael Doughty, Clerk of the Kitchen in Derby's household. Carey recommended that his brother, who was one of the yeomen waiters, should be arrested and questioned. The sequel might have been interesting because this was the same Michael Doughty (Cecilian M.P. for Liverpool) who later deposited in the custody of Egerton a trunkful of Stanley papers, sowed up in packcloth and sealed. It does not appear that Carey's suggestion was followed up.

Instead there was an official report on the presumptions of witchcraft: how a tall stranger had crossed the Earl's path twice and then the Earl fell ill; how a crone had asked about the Earl's water and the Earl's water then stopped; how a wax figure with a hair through its belly had been found in the Earl's chamber, and so on. Camden is right, no doubt, when he says that this evidence was framed to obscure the real issue. But the interesting thing is that it was accepted without question by Stow (1605) and without a breath of suspicion against the Catholics. Why then did Camden later reject it, and propound the version that Ferdinando had been poisoned by the Jesuits? The answer is very revealing.

The Cecils evidently toyed with two stories about Ferdinando, about his disgrace and about his death, which were discordant both with each other and with the witchcraft report. There was Burghley's draft of late 1594 which alleged Ferdinando's conspiracy with Catholic exiles, and so accounted for his disgrace, though it said nothing about his death. It is certain that this was never published. Then there was a later propaganda-piece, *The Estate of English Fugitives* (preserved, along with some letters to Burghley, in an Appendix to the *Sadler Papers*); this cleverly confused Ferdinando's disgrace and his death in the one word "fall," and so was able to skate over his disgrace and hint that his death was due to the exiles. There is no evidence, however, that this was publicised at the time. Lord Burghley had no wish to provoke further hatred and contempt of the Government in

Lancashire, or to let loose on himself another of those slashing responses from overseas. Very wisely, he decided to stick to the witchcraft report, a safe neutral production, readily acceptable by both Catholics and Protestants, as it was by Stow up to 1605.[1]

But by 1608, when Camden was assembling materials supplied by Burghley, the situation was very different. The Hesketh affair was quite forgotten. There had been a Gunpowder Plot. It was safe to say anything as long as it was against the Jesuits. So the lie revived and flourished.

A conservative inference from the Cecils' early manipulation of the evidence would be that they were afraid of being thought guilty of Ferdinando's death. It is hardly worth inquiring whether they were actually guilty or not, because they had such extensive time and power to obliterate any evidence of it. But the modern historian who repeats the charge that Ferdinando was poisoned should realise against whom his charge most ominously rebounds. He may then be glad to fall back on the report of the physicians who ascribed the Earl's illness to over-exercise (cf. *Appendix*.) They may well have been right.

Modern medical science, going solely on this report, would diagnose a burst appendix resulting in acute peritonitis. That, of course, was incurable till the rise of modern surgery; the frequent clysters ordered by the doctors, consisting as they did of mercury in the form of calomel, would have increased the inflammation and made death inevitable.

It must be confessed that, after all our piling-up of motives, this comes as something of an anticlimax. Those who do not wish to leave the chase without a beast in view might reply that the symptoms of acute peritonitis are difficult to distinguish from those of poisoning by arsenic or some other irritant; and that, after the initial poison had been expelled by purges, mercury in the form of corrosive sublimate might have been introduced through the clyster. But that is only conjecture; and in default of evidence—which would have

---

[1] In the decade 1587–97, prosecutions for witchcraft on the Home Circuit reached the highest point ever known in our history. Ewen, *op. cit.*, p. 110.

been obliterated if it ever existed—the conclusion must be that there is no "case for the coroner" in the physician's report. Apart from motive, the only grounds for suspicion lie in the mention of those well-known antidotes, Bezoar stone and powdered rhinoceros-horn, which show that poison *was* suspected despite the doctors' reticence; and in Sir George Carey's "vehement suspicion" against a member of the Lathom household who might possibly have tampered with the clysters; there is also a story of a silver basin stained irremediably with acid; and finally there is the fact that there were alchemists available, skilled in concealing and confusing the effects of poison. Indeed, if this were a detective-story, one could end with a glimpse of the pair that have been distantly shadowed throughout this study as instrumental villains: the familiars of Doctor Dee, Bartholomew and William Hickman, riding north a fortnight before the Earl fell ill.

March 23rd. I gave Barthilmew Hikman the nag which the Lord Keeper had given me. Barthilmew Hikman and William his brother went homeward.

There might be more to know about William Hickman. Why did the gentlemen of Lincolnshire, when he bought a house there for himself in 1598, so violently resent his presence? Why did Topcliffe (who knew some of the Shrewsbury's dark secrets) start attacking him in a way that needed Cecil's interference to stop? I confess I have not bothered to discover. The conclusion would be the same in any case.

We have no right to accuse anyone of *murdering* Ferdinando. We have every right, on the other hand, to conclude that in the Hesketh Plot and its sequel there was a determined and successful campaign to *eliminate* him as a political factor.

It is true that the Queen seemed to favour him. Twice at least she intervened on his behalf. But with Essex, the paramount favourite, and Cecil, the indispensable administrator, both against him, it was unlikely she would do anything more. She had to take the rough with the smooth; and from now on it was to be mainly rough.

"When the moon shone we did not see the candle." But, as the moon waned, she may have looked back on him with regret as a last bright taper of feudal loyalty. "So shines a good deed in a naughty world." It was a new, encroaching world, in which, as she herself lamented, "the wit of the fox is everywhere on foot, so as hardly a faithful or virtuous man may be found."

Sir Christopher Blount

THE name of Sir Christopher Blount occurs in many different fields of Elizabethan research both literary and historical.

Because of his connection with Robert Poley, who was a spy in the Babington Plot and was later present at the death of Christopher Marlowe, Blount figures in the numerous books that have been written on both those subjects. He figures also in biographies of the Earl of Leicester because he "commanded his Lordship's horse-band" and married somewhat precipitately his Lordship's widow; and in biographies of the Earl of Essex because he took a prominent part in the Cadiz expedition, in the Irish wars against Tyrone and in the disastrous rebellion of 1601. He enters the fringe of Shakespearean studies because he was among those who persuaded the Lord Chamberlain's players to act *Richard the Second* on the fateful eve of 8 February 1601. He was executed shortly afterwards and is said on good authority to have died a Catholic.

Now, there was a Catholic Christopher Blount who was brought up at the English Colleges overseas between 1562 and 1577. Is he the same person as the colourful and dashing figure whose career has just been outlined? At first it would seem not. The sole authority on Sir Christopher's parentage and early life is Sir Sidney Lee in *D.N.B.* who says nothing about his upbringing and supposes him to have been a younger brother of Charles Blount, the famous Lord Mountjoy, born in 1563.[1]

Clearly a younger brother of Mountjoy (born 1563) cannot have been overseas in 1562. Lee's supposition has passed unchallenged in all—except one—of the subsequent accounts of

[1] Dictionary of National Biography (*D.N.B.*), 11, p. 707.

115

Blount. "Other historians," as the exception, Mr Cyril Falls, observes in his *Elizabeth's Irish Wars*, "have clearly avoided the issue and make no suggestions." Mr Falls then supplies the information that Sir Christopher had a brother Sir Edward who was a *cousin* of Mountjoy and that therefore the supposition in *D.N.B.* must be abandoned. He does not himself proceed any further in the matter. But his information supplies the necessary clue.

There is no doubt that Sir Edward and Sir Christopher were brothers.[1] They campaigned together in Ireland where Edward received his knighthood. Moreover, there was, within the relevant period, only one *Sir* Christopher Blount, knighted in the Low Countries in 1588, and only one Sir Edward Blount, knighted in Dublin in 1599. Finally, this one and only Sir Edward has left behind him tangible evidence of his identity and origin. He built the almshouses at Kidderminster and was buried in the parish church there in 1630. He was the son of Thomas Blount of Kidderminster Manor who was buried there also in 1568.[2] This, then, was Christopher's parentage. There is additional evidence, from quite a different part of the country, in Berry's Hampshire pedigrees. Dealing with Richard Cotton of Warblington, who was of the same generation as Christopher and Edward, he has the following

> Richard Cotton married Elizabeth, sister of Sir Edward Blount and Sir Christopher Blount of Kidderminster.[3]

The Kidderminster Blounts were of the Worcestershire branch descended from Sir John of Sodington. Their cousinship with Mountjoy cannot have been a very close one. But

[1] Cyril Falls, *Elizabeth's Irish Wars* (London, 1950), p. 281. Mr Falls quotes letters to Cecil from Mountjoy, 21 February 1600, about his cousin Sir Edward Blount, and from Fenton, 28 February 1600, mentioning "Sir Edward Blount brother to Sir Christopher Blount"; but he has omitted the reference; it is not in the Hatfield Calendar. There is, however a reference independent of this to "Sir Chris. Blount and his brother Sir Edward"—*Calendar of State Papers Domestic*, 1598–61, p. 585, 14 February 1601.)
The reference for their knighthoods is W. A. Shaw, *The Knights of England*, (London, 1906), 11, 87, 24.
[2] Victoria County History, Worcestershire, 111, p. 169.
[3] W. Berry, *Pedigrees of familes of the County of Hants* (1833), p. 52.

all the Blounts, whether of Worcestershire or Staffordshire were keenly aware of their common descent from Sir Robert le Blond who came over with the Conqueror.

The Worcestershire Blounts figure prominently in the lists of recusants. In 1577 "Mrs Blunt widowe of Kidderminster" is in a special list along with her daughter Mrs Heath of Alvechurch and with the Throckmortons of Coughton. A later list of 1588 includes "Mr Blunt of Kidderminster," presumably her son Edward or an elder brother.[1] In the 1592 recusant roll there is a Thomas Blount of Asteley and Glashampton, a Thomas Blount of Alvechurch, and a Thomas Blount of Iddlicott in Warwickshire.[2] Sir E. K. Chambers in his *William Shakespeare* has a genealogical chart which shows all these families closely related.[3] His interest is not in the Blounts but in the families of Combe and Reynolds who intermarried with them. Joyce Blount, aunt to Edward and Christopher, was mother of the John Combe who left money to Shakespeare in his will; and another Joyce Blount, her first-cousin, was grandmother of William Reynolds to whom Shakespeare left money in his will. It is not without interest that Sir Christopher, when he helped to commission *Richard the Second* in February 1601, had probably a personal and family acquaintance with its author.

These Blounts, along with their dependents, the Combe and Reynolds families, were predominantly Catholic and recusant. It is not difficult, therefore, to see Christopher Blount of Kidderminster as the same boy who was sent overseas for his schooling.

It must be admitted, however, that the evidence for his presence overseas as early as 1562 is not altogether satisfactory. There is a passage in the life of Cardinal Allen by Nicholas Fitzherbert:

> During this period a noble English youth who had been entrusted to Allen's care at Louvain was wasting away with disease. Allen nursed him so devotedly that he contracted the same disease . . .[4]

[1] *C.R.S.*, XXII, pp. 66, 125.
[2] *C.R.S.*, XVIII, pp. 345, 358–67.
[3] E. K. Chambers, *William Shakespeare* (Oxford, 1930), II, p. 137.
[4] T. F. Knox, *Letters and Memorials of Cardinal Allen* (London, 1882), p. 5.

And to this note has been added that the noble English youth was Christopher Blount; but it is not clear whether this information comes from the Fitzherbert manuscript or merely from the modern editor, T. F. Knox. Knox amplifies the note very confidently in his introduction to the *Douai Diaries*:

> He (Allen) also acted as tutor to a young English gentleman, Christopher Blount who became well known in after years at the court of Queen Elizabeth, and died in 1600 on the scaffold in the conspiracy of the Earl of Essex.[1]

The period referred to by Fitzherbert and Knox was 1562, the date of Allen's illness. If Blount was a youth with a tutor at that date, he can scarcely have been born later than 1555. But there is more reliable evidence of Blount's presence overseas which does not agree so well with such an early date. In the lists of Englishmen who matriculated at Douai the name *Christopherus Blunt* occurs with six others in the year 1577. Of these six the ages of two can be checked: Ralph Bickley and Thomas Vavasour were both aged twenty, and that appears to be the average for other years.[2] This would suggest that Blount was born about 1557.

However that may be, there is no reason to doubt that *Christopherus Blunt* of Douai was the same as Christopher Blount of Kidderminster. Two entries in the Douai Diaries for 1576 are a confirmation. The background to them needs a brief explanation, because it contains pointers to a later unexplored period in Blount's life.

The English College at Douai was breaking up in November 1576 owing to the spread of revolt against Spain. But it was not until May 1578 that it finally settled down in its new refuge at Rheims. In the intervening period the students did a good deal of travelling to and fro. Some of them were "divines" aiming at the priesthood; others were simply boys who were there for the schooling. There is no other Blount with a different christian name mentioned in the *Diaries* of this period; so that the following entry for the 4 November may be taken as referring to Christopher:

[1] T. F. Knox, *First and Second Diaries of the English College, Douay* (London, 1878), Introduction, xxii–xxiii.　　　　　　[2] Ibid.

A servant sent by the noble lady Mrs Blunt found his way to her son who is living with us. A day or two later the servant returned to Paris ("to England" erased) accompanied by her son Mr Blunt and also Mr Throckmorton.[1]

It will be remembered that "Mrs Blunt widow of Kidderminster" was in the same special list as the Throckmortons in the recusancy returns for 1577. Evidently the servant was sent to bring Blount and Throckmorton back to their homes which were in the same part of England. But they seem to have remained in Paris for the time being.

There were two Throckmortons at Douai at this time, younger brothers of Robert, the heir to Coughton.[2] The elder of the two was Thomas who matriculated at Douai about 1574; he was later a confederate of Morgan and Paget, the originators of the Babington Plot. The younger brother was Francis Throckmorton who was executed in England in 1584 for an earlier conspiracy by the same plotters. The conjunction of the names Blount and Throckmorton is worth bearing in mind, because the only authority for the unexplored period in Blount's life is the correspondence of Thomas Morgan who has just then been mentioned.

There is one more reference to Blount in an entry of 10 November 1576, a further description of the exodus from Douai. It is of interest for several reasons, not least because it shows that he was studying for the priesthood and was fairly near to ordination:

In the last few days because of threatening dangers there have left us, some for Paris, some for England, the following whose names are here given:[3]

In the list among "students of theology" is the name of *Dominus Blount*. Among those who were still schoolboys are listed: "Master Southwell, Master Throckmorton . . . the brothers Cotton . . . ." Another of the schoolboys, though not in this list, was Gilbert Gifford. All these names have an interest in connection with Blount. Master Throckmorton was Francis already mentioned. The "brothers Cotton"

[1] T. F. Knox, *First and Second Diaries of the English College, Douay* (London, 1878), p. 112.
[2] Ibid., p. 98.   [3] Ibid., p. 113.

119

were Richard and John of Warblinton, Hants, the elder of whom married Blount's sister according to Berry's pedigree. "Master Southwell," a cousin of the Cottons, was Robert Southwell the future poet and martyr. Gilbert Gifford, by contrast, was to be the traitor and *provocateur* of the Babington Plot. Another family of Giffords who also figure in the Plot are mentioned a little further on in the *Douai Diaries*: William and his brothers Richard and George. The Giffords were cousins of the Throckmortons.

Apart from the notice of his matriculation in 1577, there is no further reference to Christopher Blount in the *Douai Diaries*.

There follows a gap of eight years. Then, in 1585, his name begins to occur in Morgan's intercepted correspondence with Mary Queen of Scots. If it were not for this evidence there would be nothing to connect the outlawed Catholic seminarist of 1577 with the dashing Protestant captain who was knighted in 1588. As it is, the connection is like a dotted line, with many gaps, yet pointing in one direction.

Thomas Morgan was Mary's agent at Paris with the French court. He was also the leader (along with Charles Paget) of those Catholics who were hostile to Dr Allen, the future Cardinal, and to his colleges at Rheims and Rome.[1] Among his followers were the clerics Gilbert and William Gifford and the Throckmortons, Thomas and Francis—names which it will be remembered, go back to Blount's Douai days. One of the points at issue between Allen and Morgan was how best to serve the Scottish Queen. Allen, who was the true representative of the English Catholics abroad, was sternly opposed to Morgan's entertainment of dubious adventurers like George Gifford and William Parry who offered to assassinate Queen Elizabeth.[2] Such intrigues, he warned Morgan, were

[1] For the connection between Morgan's quarrels and the Babington Plot, see J. H. Pollen, *Mary Stuart and the Babington Plot* (Edinburgh, 1922), Introduction, and Conyers Read, *Mr Secretary Walsingham* (Oxford, 1925), the end of Vol. II and beginning of Vol. III.

[2] For George Gifford, see J. H. Pollen, *op. cit.*, 169–75: and in *The Month*, XCIX, p. 607.

For the "Parry Plot," see Leo Hicks, "The strange case of William Parry," *Studies* (Dublin), September 1948.

much more dangerous to the Scottish than to the English Queen. This was proved by the outcome of the "Parry Plot." Early in 1585 Mary was moved to Tutbury under the fanatical supervision of Sir Amyas Paulet, and all her intercourse with the outside world was rigidly sealed off.

As a result of the same plot Morgan had to undergo a light imprisonment in Paris. But this did not prevent him from continuing to be a centre of intrigue. In January 1585, hearing of Mary's move to Tutbury, he wrote to Christopher Blount in the hope of establishing through him a secret means of communication.[1] It is thus, from a biographical point of view, that Morgan supplies the link between Blount the seminarist and Blount the soldier—by way of Blount the spy. Some of Morgan's associates were genuine devotees of Mary, as Francis Throckmorton had been. But others, notably Gilbert Gifford and his cousin George Gifford, were the conscious instruments of her ruin. It remains to be seen in which category Christopher Blount should be placed.

Morgan's first dealings with Blount are described by him in a letter to Mary of 10 July 1585, in which it is stated that Blount is a servant of the Earl of Leicester, and it is implied that he is still a Catholic and that he is living in Staffordshire in the vicinity of Tutbury. Blount had replied to him (says Morgan) declaring his devotion to Mary "the only saint that he knows living upon the ground," and promising to establish intelligence with her. The bearer of his reply from England to Paris was "a gentleman named Robert Poley." Morgan then assured Mary that Blount and Poley had joined Leicester's service from the highest motives; they "followed Leicester in the hope of quietness and being able thereby to live a Christian life."

Poley, however, was in fact one of those "intelligencers" whom great men used to do their dirty work. He had been connected with Leicester—if he is the "Master Pooley" of *Leicester's Commonwealth*—as early as 1578. In 1584 he had emerged from a light prison-sentence, professing himself a

[1] Morgan to Mary, 10/20 July 1585. The letter is printed in full in Murdin, *State Papers*, 1759, p. 446, and summarised in the Calendar of MSS at Hatfield (*Hatf. Cal.*), p. 101.

Catholic and seeking to mingle with recusant society. But his private life was thoroughly disreputable and he was an object of distrust to all sincere Catholics.[1] Morgan, however, continued to think well of him despite many warnings.

Whether or not Poley was the bearer of this letter of July 1585, it is certain that the letter passed into the hands of Walsingham; for no secret letters reached Mary between March 1585 and January 1586, and those that then began to reach her were instruments in the scheme to ruin her; they had all been intercepted and copied by Phelippes, Walsingham's handwriting expert. It is plain, therefore, that Blount's dealings with Morgan were known to Walsingham before the end of 1585. Yet he did not suffer the fate of Francis Throckmorton. His career was not interrupted by imprisonment and torture; instead he proceeded to Holland at the end of the year in Leicester's retinue.

In spite of his absence in Holland, Morgan and Paget wrote to Mary in the new year saying that both Blount and Poley were working in her interests.[2] There is also the suggestion that Blount could be used to convey letters into Scotland. The suggestion about letters for Scotland is also continued in a note from Phelippes to Walsingham, 19 March 1586; but Poley, not Blount, is the man mentioned by Phelippes as the intended bearer.[3] There is little doubt that Poley, whatever his original intentions, was by this time working for the Government; he had been placed in the household of Lady Sidney, which brought him directly under the control of Walsingham, Lady Sidney's father. Morgan, however, still believed (or affected to believe) that Poley was hoodwinking Walsingham and acting as a spy for Mary.

The question of Morgan's guilt or innocence in Mary's destruction is obviously outside the competence of this article. The only question to be investigated is whether Blount was a renegade.

There are two grave reasons for thinking that he was. In

[1] For Poley's character and reputation, see the narrative of William Weston, quoted by Pollen, *op. cit.*, pp. cxxii–iii; also F. S. Boas, *Christopher Marlowe and his circle* (Oxford, 1929), 32–4.

[2] *Hatf. Cal.*, III, 130, 135.

[3] See J. Morris, *Sir Amias Poulet* (London, 1874), p. 156.

the first place, instead of suffering for his complicity, he prospered. In the second place, he corresponded with Poley as late as 1588—that is to say, at a time when Poley's treachery was taken for granted by all Catholics.[1]

On the other hand it is not at first clear what part, if any, he played in Walsingham's complicated scheme for enticing Mary into a framed conspiracy. The chief agent in this was Gilbert Gifford. In December 1585, with the full confidence of Morgan and Paget, Gifford had come across from Paris to London where he lodged with Phelippes, Walsingham's agent. In London he received powers from Walsingham to command the full co-operation of Sir Amyas Paulet, Mary's gaoler; armed with these powers he proceeded to Chartley, near Tutbury, whither Mary had recently been moved. His own house, an ancient and honourable one, was about ten miles from Chartley. By his great powers of deception and by his local influence he built up an organisation for sending secret letters to Tutbury.

In January 1586 Mary got her first batch of letters from Morgan, those written by him in the previous year; they included the one of July recommending Blount and Poley, and a later one of October recommending Gilbert Gifford. Mary was delighted at this seeming turn of fortune. It only now remained for Gifford to persuade her to entrust her outgoing letters to the same organisation.

It may be that Mary's reception of Morgan's letter brought her first awareness of Blount's existence. On the other hand it is possible that he had made his presence known to her before March 1585 when Paulet shut her off from the world. In either case his Catholic intercedents were such as to tempt her confidence. Morgan continued to recommend him to her in letters of March and July 1586: as "a gentleman of good house, discreet and valiant."[2] It is these letters that suggest that Blount may indeed have played a part in the organisation of Gifford, Paulet and Walsingham.

On 31 March Morgan wrote to her that it was thought necessary to recall Christopher Blount out of Holland, and

[1] The evidence for this and its documentation is given by F. S. Boas, *op. cit.*, pp. 31, 54.   [2] *Hatf. Cal.*, III, 137, 151.

that this would be possible because of his credit with his cousin Charles Blount (later Lord Mountjoy) who was Elizabeth's new favourite. On 10 July he wrote again, mentioning Blount for the last time; he said that he was to be entrusted with Mary's letters for Scotland. It is possible, though not obligatory, to read these letters as information that Blount would be in England about March and leaving again about July. It is tempting to read them in this sense, because there is evidence from the other side of the conspiracy, from Paulet and Gifford, of a new and anonymous Government agent appearing on the scene and disappearing within just the same months; and the evidence about this anonymous figure suits no one as well as Blount.

In January 1586, as has been said, Gilbert Gifford had established his system at Chartley and was passing in letters from Morgan. But before Mary would put complete trust in the system, it was necessary that she should see it approved by the French Ambassador. For this and other reasons Gifford left his post near Chartley and returned to France. In his place a person referred to as "the Substitute" was appointed.

To find this substitute cannot have been easy. Although Mary was at the mercy of untrustworthy adherents, she was still difficult to deceive; she refused for example to make any use of Poley despite Morgan's recommendations. The substitute had to be someone whose antecedents she could trust, as she trusted Gifford because of his honoured name and his relationship with Francis Throckmorton who had died in her cause. The substitute had also to be someone whose fidelity (or treachery rather) Walsingham could guarantee to the grim and suspicious Paulet.

But in addition he had to have a third qualification which, trifling though it sounds, was essential to the scheme. He had to be *persona grata* to the local brewer who was the actual instrument for taking the letters in and out of Chartley. Although the brewer was taking money from both sides, it was necessary that he should believe that the person to whom he handed Mary's letters was one of her true supporters. The reason for this is not clear, but it is reiterated several times in letters to Walsingham both by Gifford and by Paulet.

Blount, by his name and acquaintance with the Throckmortons, had the first qualification; his service under Leicester guaranteed him the second; and if he had established himself in the locality early in 1585 as a secret supporter of Mary, then he already possessed the third.

On 10 March, Paulet wrote to Walsingham describing his satisfaction with the substitute. The first line of his letter applies to no known person so well as to Blount:

> Choice is made of a substitute of honest credit, good wealth, good understanding, and a servant to the Earl of Leicester, from whom I look hourly to hear of the delivery of the first packet according to the direction received from you . . .[1]

The packet was from the French Ambassador. The trap was now set at both ends. How Babington was enticed to walk into the other end of it need not be related here.

The task of the "Substitute" ended when Gilbert Gifford returned to Chartley in June. Gifford appointed a "second substitute", a cousin of his, who was directly under his orders. The first and original substitute, however, seems to have played his part well; for Gifford wrote to Phelippes on 7 July that he had had to bribe the brewer again to transfer his confidence from the first to the second:

> . . . I think he is sufficiently charmed for admitting any other but "the first man."[2]

As regards the identity of the second substitute there have been several guesses by historians.[3] But the anonymity of the first and original substitute has so far remained intact.

Whether or not he was Christopher Blount, there is one last piece of evidence that Blount was an accomplice of some kind. It is an attestation by Curle, Mary's secretary, that in a letter intended for use at her trial a paragraph mentioning Blount and Poley had been omitted.[4] When this point is

---

[1] See J. Morris, *op. cit.*, p. 154.

[2] J. H. Pollen, *op. cit.*, 103. But Fr. Pollen seems to have misunderstood this letter.

[3] His pseudonym was usually "Barnaby". Lingard thought he was Thomas Throckmorton. Conyers Read is surely right in refusing Pollen's identification of him with the cheap spy, Thomas Barnes. My own choice would be *George* Gifford, who possessed the same qualifications as Blount and was Gilbert's cousin.   [4] See J. Morris, *op. cit.*, p. 118, note 6.

added to the two already mentioned—Blount's rising fortunes and his later correspondence with Poley—there is a strong case that he played the part of a false friend and *provocateur*.

In the autumn of 1586, when the Babington Plot was flaring up and the Scottish Queen was doomed, Blount obtained what had probably been his heart's desire all the time: he was made a lieutenant in an auxillary troop of Leicester's horse, 150 lances.[1] In November came the incident which opened an entirely new phase in his career. At the foray at Zutphen he charged with Sir Philip Sidney and the young Earl of Essex and fought with a valour worthy of that bright and futile episode. According to Essex, he rescued Sir Francis Vere from a ring of Spaniards when his horse was slain.[2] A year or two later he was knighted on the field of battle, and is thereafter described as "Captain of his lordship's horseband." In 1589, shortly after Leicester's death he married his widowed countess as her third husband. She was Letitia Knollys, previously Countess of Essex. Blount thus became the stepfather of his new friend and patron, the young Earl of Essex. Letitia was fifty, Blount in his early thirties. The marriage, which caused some scandal, probably ended Blount's hope of success as a courtier, for Letitia was *anathema* to Elizabeth I. But his fortune as a soldier and a country gentleman were assured as long as Essex's star was in the ascendant.

In 1592, by Essex's favour, he established his right to an estate designated as "Ulceter (i.e. Uttoxeter) Moors." It will be remembered that Morgan's letter of 1585 implied that Blount was living in the vicinity of Tutbury and Chartley (which were joined to each other by the road through Uttoxeter). It is likely that the estate was part of the patrimony of the recusant Walter Blount who forfeited it some time before Michaelmas 1585 and remained in prison for his religion until the end of the reign.[3] The Blounts took a long view of their family claims.[4]

[1] *Hatf. Cal.*, III, p. 457.   [2] *Hatf. Cal.*, VI, p. 570.
[3] *D.N.B.*, II, p. 707. *C.R.S.*, XVIII, p. 296, and II, pp. 231–88.
[4] For example Sir Edward Blount willed Kidderminster to his distant relative, Mountjoy's son; Sir Michael Blount, of the remote Oxfordshire branch, made an unsuccessful claim to the Mountjoy title and estate.

Christopher's subsequent rise to be a Colonel and then Master of Horse under Essex need not detain us, while his part in the Essex rebellion would need a close examination of that ambiguous episode than is possible here. What matters for the present biography is that his early beliefs and training proved in the end too strong for him to resist.[1]

He was reconciled with the Church in Ireland by the Jesuit Fr Fitzsimon in 1598; and thereafter he actively practised his religion, to the extent of trying to convert others. Had he been wholly guided by the Jesuits he would indeed have taken no part in the Essex rebellion. But on the other hand it is quite possible that up to the end he was reluctant; his last escapade in the street-fighting may have been simply the desperation of one who knew that he was trapped in any case. He was in the same *impasse* to which, fifteen years earlier, he had helped to bring the unfortunate young associates of Anthony Babington. It may not be altogether fanciful to regard it as a sort of expiation.

He was almost certainly made a scapegoat to some extent, and his religion singled him out for especially virulent accusations by Sir Robert Cecil at the trial. Francis Bacon, however, who conducted the prosecution, pronounced what may be considered a juster epitaph:

"Sir Christopher Blount, so enterprising and prodigal of his own life . . ."[2]

[1] The remaining facts are taken from D.N.B., II, p. 707.

[2] ADDENDUM. In view of Blount's general reputation for valour and generosity, a more favourable construction might be placed on his actions in 1585–6. While it is certain that his first step in sending Poley to Morgan was the beginning of great harm to the Scottish Queen, it might be possible to exonerate him from the crime of personal treachery along the following lines:

He is solicited gratuitously by Morgan whom he knows to be a trouble-maker. He takes the   :er to Leicester protesting his desire to keep clear from all such intrigues. Leicester tells him not to worry, to leave all to him. Leicester then instructs Poley and Blount fades out of the picture.

Morgan's repeated assertions of Blount's devotion to Mary may have had no foundation outside Poley's inventive mind. Blount's correspondence with Poley in 1588 may signify no more than an attempt by Poley to blackmail him in his prosperity.

The Unwilling Apostate

The Case of Anthony Tyrrell

THERE was something about Anthony Tyrrell that kept leading him to the brink of high tragedy, and then plunging him instead into farce. Even his extremely distinguished lineage could not escape a faint note of ridicule. His uncanny facility for catching the eye of important persons, with unfortunate consequences, might almost have been hereditary. The progenitor of the family was that Sir Walter who is gratefully remembered by children as having shot William Rufus in mistake for a stag. Another ancestor, Sir James, was chosen by Richard Crouchback to suffocate the Princes in the Tower. It is at least true that the Tyrrells had a strong tradition of personal loyalty to the Crown. Sir Henry, fourteenth knight in descent from Sir Walter, compromised with the Elizabethan Settlement and hoped for better days. But his brother George was one of that company of sad gentlemen—very different from the fierce Geneva exiles—who took their consciences into obscurity abroad and left their hearts behind. By 1573 he was so poor that he had to travel on foot, carrying his luggage. It was a doleful youth-time for Anthony, his eldest son, who had left elmy England with his father at the age of eight.

In 1573 Anthony, being now twenty-one, came back secretly to England, with half a crown in his pocket, to solicit alms from his numerous relatives. Some prettily-phrased begging letters and a sheet of verses were found on him when he was arrested. If each relative, he argued, would give him a little, he would soon accumulate the ten pounds necessary for completing his studies. He had accumulated some old clothes and a promise of four pounds when he came to grief with his aunt, Lady Petre of Ingatestone. One of the letters described in doggerel:

> ... the entertainment we had at Ingerstone, the which because it was not very good beshrew Mrs. Jones—We came in I think a saturnical hour, for the old drab began upon us so to lower—that although she were my aunt Rebecca's maid, her look would have made the devil himself afraid. ...

An ex-minister, bearing the memorable name of Davy Jones—perhaps the husband of Aunt Rebecca's maid—had been released from the stocks in order to supply Walsingham with intimate details about the Tyrrells and neighbouring families. He had gone through a form of conversion to the Catholic Faith, and this enabled him to sponge on his victims as well as to extract a pittance for his information from Mr Mills, Walsingham's secretary. This creature was probably the instrument of Anthony's apprehension.

The verses which were found on him when he was arrested are worth transcribing; though trivial, they sound more sea-worthy than the average pre-Spenserian construction:

> Like as the merchant, which on surging seas
> In beaten bark hath felt the grievous rage
> Of Aeolus' blasts, till Neptune for his ease
> By princely powers their choler did assuage:
> 　　　　　　　　Even so my muse
> Doth seem by Fortune's cruel spite
> To feel her cup so mixed with bitter gall
> As no conceit could make her to delight,
> Until she chanced in scholarship to fall
> 　　　　　　　　With you, my friend,
> Whom mighty Jove hath sent me for relief
> When heavy cares would seek for to appese
> My pensive mind, and slyly as a thief
> Hold me captivèd still in sore distress.

Unwittingly prophetic, the poor scholar was held captivèd still in sore distress for two years. There was little persecution-to-death at this time. It is true that a simple and saintly priest, Father Wodehouse (pronounced "Wuddus"), had been very brutally executed in the previous year. But that was partly because he got Lord Burghley on the raw. He insisted first on addressing him as "William Cecil"; then began patiently to explain the catechism to him as to a child; finally when Burghley, exchanging wrath for guile, or mockery, offered him a post as his chaplain, he accepted eagerly and asked at what hour Burghley would be ready to be confessed and receive absolution.

Burghley's notorious snobbery, which helped Father Wuddus to heaven, helped Anthony into the wide world again. There was intercession by relatives, and a humbled but very noble letter from old George Tyrrell. Burghley liked to offset Walsingham's brusquerie with the old nobility; and to have a scion of sheer Norman stock, gracefully suppliant on the carpet before him, was soothing balm. Anthony by all inferences was a charmer, and it is likely that he made various promises he had no very firm intention of keeping. He was released in 1576—perhaps only just in the nick of time. For in that year came the first alarums of invading "Seminaries." Allen's overseas foundations of Rheims and Rome were issuing their challenge, and the great battle for the soul of England, which was to engage most of Burghley's attention for the rest of the century, had begun.

To Rome Anthony betook himself. By 1581—in too short a time—he was ordained priest. He crossed over to England, for the second time, in the wake of Campion's great band of martyrs. He was caught again, and now, for certain, he stood on the threshold of martyrdom. But with the aid of a resourceful companion he broke prison in 1582 and, sheltered by illustrious Catholics, escaped abroad again. He was thirty now, talented, popular, and priested, with the halo of near-martyrdom. He applied for admission to the Society of Jesus, but was not accepted. His companion of the prison exploit, an older and worldlier man—his name was Ballard—now introduced him to quite a different set of Catholic exiles: the Paget-Morgan crowd, who hob-nobbed with French *politiques*, disparaged Dr Allen, and thought the Jesuits a menace to society. To this time probably belong the following reflections, penned later, on an old and well-known theme:

But among all other things one of the principal causes of my spoiling was in not keeping my heart pure and clean as at the beginning it was; and long had the enemy practised with me to desire to be conversant

130

much with women, and this under the colour of holiness and piety; who of themselves although they were very good and vertuous, yet did my soul often catch deformity before that ever I departed their company.[1]

Tyrrell could write. But a life of excitement and intrigue now opened up before him. Ballard appeared one day early in 1585 resplendently disguised as Captain Fortescue, a military man. He was going to England on a mission of momentous importance. Tyrrell, lightheartedly daring as usual, set sail with him. Actually, the mission was a confidence trick along the usual lines; a rising of Catholic gentry in England was to be kindled by assurances of a French (alternatively of a Spanish) invasion; then a Spanish (alternatively a French) invasion was to be stimulated by reports of an imminent *coup d'état* in England. It was not long before Tyrrell began to see through the older man's magniloquence and to laugh secretly at him; all the same, it was fun to swagger about in fine clothes and to enjoy, even in a backstairs way, his birthright as a courtier:

> I began to be in expenses, not considering that I lived upon the alms of other men. Then fell I to haunt taverns and ordinaries far unfit for my profession, to spend with the best, to ride up and down upon pleasure only, and to slack the spiritual harvest. Alms given to me only to bestow I would oftentimes hold and reserve some part myself, under the colour of necessity, whereby the spirit of covetousness got hold of me, and then I was sore assailed with pride, covetousness, gluttony and lechery. What shall I say more?

Living handsomely upon alms, they toured the country houses of England, with a personal attendant called Mr Maude. This gentleman sent back conscientious reports on their itinerary to Sir Francis Walsingham. The country squires, one is glad to note, received them with increasing coldness. But Ballard made a great hit, at first, among the young gentlemen of the Inns of Court and of the Queen's Bodyguard:

[1] Tyrrell's manuscript, edited by Robert Persons, was first published together with the autobiography of William Weston, by Morris, *The Troubles of Our Catholic Forefathers*, ii (London, 1875). In this book Fr Morris cites other sources for a life of Anthony Tyrrell. But further information, not available to him, is contained in Boyd, *Calendar of Scottish Papers*, viii (for the Babington Plot) and in the *Hatfield Calendar*, iv (for the episode of 1593.)

Fortescue had his attendants as thick as might be, every gentleman calling him Captain, insomuch that in every tavern and inn in London he was called Captain Fortescue, and every man thought that knew him not, that he with a great band should have gone over with my Lord of Leicester.

Ballard, though a bombastic mischief-making dupe, was at least an honest partisan. But behind him Tyrrell had glimpses of a much more unsavoury type of political ecclesiastic. Of this type were the two Giffords: Dr William, a sinister fool, and his cousin Gilbert, a baby-faced devil; it was through them that the idea of assassinating Queen Elizabeth became part of the "Babington Plot"; and yet they were at the same time negotiating with Walsingham for the overthrow of the Jesuits and Seminary Priests who obeyed Dr Allen. This two-facedness was, with them, the art of the professional "intelligencer." But, in the case of Tyrrell, it simply aggravated his natural ambivalence; while he was consciously carrying out his spiritual duties as a priest, he was sub-consciously brooding on how these might be turned to his temporal advantage as a politician, if he were captured—and capture was getting nearer and nearer.

Although the "Babington Plot" did not break open till August 1586, long lists of suspects (most of them innocent) were being drawn up by Walsingham's spies, months beforehand. As early as June there were preliminary arrests of individuals from whom incriminating evidence, true or false, might be extracted. Anthony Babington himself—whose character rather resembled Anthony Tyrrell's except that it was haughtier and less resilient—opened negotiations with Walsingham on June 29th.

But by this time—by April, in fact—Tyrrell had parted from Ballard, revived his fervour, and thrown himself into the apostolate, in company with Father Weston, the only Jesuit then in England, and a band of Seminary Priests. By a very unfortunate coincidence the apostolate was undergoing a phase which made it almost as dangerous as politics to one of Anthony's temperament. In the first half of 1586 there was a positive mania for *exorcising* hysterical persons thought to be demoniacs. These 'exorcisms,' carried out according to some quite unauthorised French ritual, were, though humanely intended, extremely grotesque and even brutal. From a modern point of view it is incredible that good and intelligent men—and so these priests were—could have indulged in them. But in fact they were simply a less cruel form of the contemporary Protestant mania for witch-hunting. With the capture of Weston and the others, the exorcisms ceased altogether; and the new Jesuit superior Garnet, who landed with Southwell in July, was certainly not the man to renew them. But in May and June they were at their height, and Tyrrell threw himself into them with abandon. He wrote a treatise on the subject, *The Book of Miracles*, which was later to enter anonymously into Shake-speare's *King Lear*. Tyrrell's association with the exorcists brought a new range of suspects into Walsingham's ken. They were closely watched, and, on July 4th, for the third time in his life, Tyrrell was apprehended.

He entered his prison cell full of buoyed-up fervour. But the two days and nights of suspense and neglect that followed caused a change of outlook. On 6 July he wrote to his old patron Lord Burghley (who had promised to be a second father to him) offering information: "of that of which your honour shall be full fain."

This change is not quite such a hopeless collapse as it seems. Among the small section of the clergy that was hostile to Cardinal Allen the custom had already begun which was to continue for the next hundred years, of bargaining with the Government along the lines of toleration for Catholics in exchange for the extermination of the Jesuits. The age was so honeycombed with double-crossing that, historically, it would not be surprising to find that Anthony had been an "intelligencer" ever since his first interview with Burghley ten years earlier. Psychologically, in his case, it is not pos-sible; but it is highly probable that in 1586 he had begun to fancy himself as one of those private detectives at large who were anxious to help the Government in accordance with some particular *nostrum* for Church and State. But to be a private detective it was essential *to be at large*. Anthony was in bonds; and he was soon made to feel that unconditional surrender was the only opening to Lord Burghley's favour. His breaking-point came in August when he was allowed to see the racked and crippled form of Ballard being carried in a chair for fresh examination. He made a formal recantation on the Genevan Bible, before Justice Young, and set himself to write whatever was required of him.

What was required of him was to answer leading questions and add corroborative detail. His accusations fell under three heads. Those against Babington's companions were of little value except in the case of a young Guardsman, Charles Tilney; Tyrrell's cowardly slanders may have tipped the scale against him. Those against the Pope and the Jesuits as authors of the murder-plot were in such contradiction with the main evidence that no use was made of them. But those against the Catholics who had sheltered and befriended him proved terribly effective and led to many executions, imprisonments, and ruinations.

In September Tyrrell was given a large measure of liberty to spy on his fellow prisoners in the Clink, and to hear their confessions; various devices were used to make it seem that he was still a firm confessor for the Faith. While he plied this dreadful trade, Charles Tilney mounted the scaffold and said to the haranguing minister: "Preacher, I have come to die, not to argue," and three priests who had been his admired fellow-workers in June, went bravely and gently, on his evidence, to the traitor's death. He was striving desperately and savagely for some recognition that would restore his self-esteem. The omens seemed propitious. Davison, the Queen's Secretary, though very busy this October, found time to write to Burghley:

> The letter from Tyrrell was very agreeable to her Majesty, both for the style and affection of the man which she greatly commendeth.

But October wore on without remuneration. Burghley and Young cast their nets wider, and turned the screw tighter. In the faces of his fellow-Catholics Tyrrell began to see the first signs of a dreadful misgiving. His reflections at this time could have supplied matter for *Faustus* and *Macbeth* more pertinent than his anonymous contribution to *King Lear*:

I thought my sins too abominable and grievous, and albeit I believed that God could forgive them, yet I assured myself that he never would do it, for I found in myself no hope or desire of amendment. My sleeps were troublesome, my dreams fearful at my going to bed. I thought it booted not to pray, and yet without prayer I thought the devil would have too much power over me. The Sign of the Cross and other customs of the Catholic Church I had laid aside, and yet at times fear forced me to use them. Truly, I do not lie. I would sometimes, when my candle was put out, imagine my chamber to be full of devils, especially of those I had tormented in my former exorcisms. I imagined how they environed me round about, triumphing of their possession of me, and watching when they should carry my soul as their perpetual prey into eternal damnation.

Yet in his day-light consciousness he still grasped at those dreams which in his days of piety had been subconscious temptations:

And yet if I had been asked that time what was the sum of all my felicity that I had proposed unto myself, forsooth I could answer no other, but only to come into favour with her Majesty, to be well thought of such as are of best account about her, to gain myself some temporal living, to get me a woman to be my concubine (for wife by reason of my priesthood she could be none), to break the vow of my holy orders, to live in all kinds of sensuality.

By Christmas time he knew for certain that he was not cut out to be a machiavel; the worm of conscience would never let him be. Blindly, faltering, starting at every shadow, he began to grope towards the light. He began to go to confession to a blind priest—but always with the half-resolution that if he were suspected he would say it was a mock-confession to entrap the priest. Still, the grace of the sacrament works if it is not positively rejected. He began to unburden himself secretly in the long series of retractations from which most of the passages quoted here are taken. The torment of this dual role became evident to his fellow-Catholics in prison. They raided his private room, and found torn copies of Burghley's letters to him with notes of his answers on the back. He was arraigned before an informal court of prisoners one night in the Marshalsea: a grim and distressing scene. This external push settled him. He was finally reconciled about the middle of February. With his reconciliation he recovered his nerve.

Correspondence between Walsingham and Phelippes,

written with controlled exasperation, gives details of his escape and directions for his recapture; it was known that he had composed "fifty sheets" which might present Lord Burghley in a most unfavourable light. In March 1587 he had been given five pounds by Justice Young, with a commission to do spy work in Norfolk. Meanwhile, with incredible generosity, his fellow-Catholics had subscribed fifty pounds for his escape. With pursuivants hard on his heels, he reached Yorkshire, worked his way across the Scottish border, and, in May, caught a fly-boat from Leith to the German shore. From there his precious 'fifty sheets" were dispatched to Father Persons in Rome. Shortly after that, he returned quietly to England and gave himself up!

Persons, who edited but did not publish his papers, does not, like a later editor, ascribe his return to another fit of back-sliding; he simply says that Tyrrell could not face a life of long and ignominious repentance. From what follows it seems clear that, with a sort of mad economy, he had decided on the only antidote that would both kill the poison of his treachery and cure his mortally-wounded self-esteem. "Your dissembling," Burghley had written in one of his letters, "is to a good end, and therefore both tolerable and commendable."[1]

Very well! he would carry his enemy's instructions one step further, and then, with one grand, heroic, sacrificial gesture, he would blow them to the moon.

Burghley seems to have betrayed no particular surprise at his return; this suggests a refinement of double-crossing too intricate to be worth unravelling. It was arranged that Tyrrell should preach a sermon of public repentance for his temporary lapse; and he was given full facilities to compose it. With inspired energy he wrote another one, at the same time, very different in tone, and made copy after copy of it. The day chosen for the ceremony was 31 January 1588; the place, Paul's Cross.

A great concourse awaited him. He was preceded by a

[1] Burghley's letters are Tyrrell's transcribed versions of them; but they can generally be checked, both in substance and in phraseology, by his answers to them which are among the State Papers.

famous preacher, John Reynolds, who bade the multitude give attentive hearing to the edifying words that were to follow. Then Anthony Tyrrell, taking a firm grip on himself and on the papers within his doublet, mounted the pulpit. He looked down on the packed crowds. This was as near to Tyburn as he would ever get—and surely it was near enough. He lifted up his head and lived his finest hour:

> The cause of my coming here this day is to protest before God and His Angels and you that are present that I am a most horrible, heinous, and detestable sinner thus to behave myself, and unworthy of all mercy and grace both before God and man; and that the true cause of my coming up to this pulpit is to confirm my first confession, made by the instinct of God's holy grace and written with mine own hand, of the most inpudent lies and wicked slanders that I uttered to the Right Honourable my Lord Treasurer and others against many innocent persons—

Of course he was interrupted almost immediately. But before he could be torn down, he had flung his copies broadcast among the crowd, where there were Catholics waiting to pick them up. The scene that followed has been described by Persons with his swift and stabbing pen:

> But in the main space all was in marvellous hurly and burly at Paul's Cross, where the people had heard three sermons in one hour, all contrary the one to the other; the first of the preacher in praise and credit of Tyrrell; the second of Tyrrell himself in derogation of the preacher; the third of Justice Young threatening death to those that should believe Tyrrell. But the concourse of people was so unruly as Tyrrell was carried away on men's shoulders to the gaol of Newgate, by St Nicholas' shambles in Newgate market, the Protestants crying out vengeance upon him, and he weeping bitterly and knocking his breast and affirming that he had done nothing that day but upon mere force and compulsion of his conscience—

and Persons concludes ominously:

> And the concourse was so great about the prison as they were forced to change him within two hours after to the Counter, where none came to him but Topcliffe and Young.

The mention of Topcliffe suggests physical torture. We do not know. We only know that he held out resolutely for three months, and then fell desperately ill. While he lay prostrate, the Spanish Armada came and went. Its failure may have had something to do with his own. He recovered his health, but his nerve had gone. On December 8th—the feast of the Conception—he read an uneventful recantation of all his former Catholic pronouncements.

Now that all the fight was knocked out of him, his captors treated him with great generosity. He was given two vicarages and a wife in his native country of Essex. Thus did the rosy fancies of his illicit dreamland become tangible fact— "to gain myself some temporal living, to get me a woman to be my concubine (for wife by reason of my priesthood she could be none)." Here, between Dengy and Southminster, he lived for the next five years; and here he might have ended his days, like a minor Herrick, writing verses, preaching occasionally on Sundays, and having mild affairs with village lasses. But the worm, the gnawing worm, would not let him be. Neither would his relatives overseas. He had a sister, a nun in the Bridgettine convent at Rouen, and some message seems to have been smuggled across which decided him to make one more bid for his salvation.

In the autumn of 1593, armed with all his realisable wealth in the form of sixty-four gold pounds, he arrived in London. His travel-agent was a certain Lieutenant Ferris who contracted to get people across from Southampton to Dieppe as part of the Earl of Essex's army. But Ferris's wife kept a brothel in Fenchurch Street; and that, as far as Tyrrell was concerned, proved the be-all and end-all of the affair. Once he got as far as Croydon, and another time to Staines, presumably on his way to the coast; but on both occasions he gravitated back to Mrs Ferris in Fenchurch Street. His money dwindled to thirty-six pounds. In September, Ferris's organisation was rounded up by the London magistrates; and, once again, after five years, Tyrrell found himself face to face with his old acquaintance, Justice Young. It was a far cry from the days when he slipped to and fro across the channel with such easy daring.

He was in no shape for heroics now; he tried to pass the whole thing off as a disreputable escapade, and gave full details of his misfortunes in the brothel. Young, who was more actively interested in Ferris, seems to have regarded

Tyrrell with feelings as near to amusement as an assumption of puritanism would permit. Indeed, from his point of view, there *was* something grimly humorous about the utter degradation of Tyrrell's excuses. While Southwell hung silent against a wall till the blood came out of his mouth, these "auricular confessions" of his fellow-priest were a compensating contrast.

But Sir Robert Cecil, who had stepped into Walsingham's place, took a more serious view. The year 1593 was one of acute rivalry between his spy organisation and that of Essex. It was also a critical year for poets; Christopher Marlowe was stabbed in 1593, Henry Constable was converted, and John Donne apostatised. Constable, with whom Tyrrell was acquainted, was one of Essex's numerous intelligencers; and Tyrrell's answers concerning him provide a useful pointer to the dating of his life. Cecil was anxious not to miss anything. By the end of November Tyrrell was still languishing in the Marshalsea in a penniless condition. Young took a paternal interest in him, and advised Cecil that he was now thoroughly penitent and might be sent home to his wife. An abject letter from Tyrrell in December confirmed this. He was sent back to his wife, or rather to his concubine—"for wife by reason of my priesthood she could be none." High tragedy had finished in low farce in a manner reminiscent of *Measure for Measure*. Having dared death a second time, like Claudio at the bidding of his sister, Tyrrell had ended up in the role of Lucio: "Marrying a punk, my lord, is pressing to death, whipping, *and* hanging."

But Shakespeare's only known acquaintance with Anthony Tyrrell was *incognito* and at second hand. It sprang from his last public appearance, in 1601, and it came about in this way. Samuel Harsnet, chaplain to the Bishop of London, had got himself into serious trouble for licensing Hayward's book on Richard the Second, and had only saved himself by crawling as abjectly as ever Tyrrell did. To recover favour he was engaged, at the bidding of his bishop, in fomenting discord among the hard-pressed Catholic minority. The line chosen, to discredit the Jesuits, was to rake up the sixteen-year-old episode of the exorcisms. The result was the book known as *A Declaration of Egregious Popish Impostures, etc.* Tyrrell, with his *Book of Miracles,* was a principal witness; but he gave his evidence with disappointing sobriety and reluctance. The star witness was a half-witted prison drab who was prevailed on to utter the usual dreary slanders against the chastity of some of the most heroic martyrs. In this form, spiced with salacity and inflated with pious bombast, the book became a best-seller in 1603; and its loud-mouthed, yellow-bellied author went on to be Archbishop of York. Today it is only remembered because Shakespeare read it and put bits of it into the mouth of Edgar—Edgar, the typical recusant—in the enigmatic way that marks his awareness of the religious conflict.

After that, Tyrrell's moth-like figure relapsed once more into the obscurity of the age whose highlights he could hit with such unerring truancy. But if he had less constancy than some, he had more than most. At least he fought with Mammon before he became its slave and echo. And there is good reason to believe that at the very end, like a wise clown, he cheated his hard master. Weston, in his memoirs written in 1615, adds that he has just heard that Tyrrell in his old age slipped across into Belgium and died at peace with the Church. This is confirmed by a list of apostate priests, preserved in the Old Chapter, which carries against the name of Anthony Tyrrell the note: *mortuus est poenitens.*

St Ambrose, on the adultery of David, says that Kings are accustomed to sin, but not accustomed to repent. It is not really surprising that one of Tyrrell's temperament, caught between the heroic discipline of the Counter-Reformation and the hard realities of Elizabethan politics, should have been mangled with such sickening results. But what is surprising is that at the end of it all, he should have crawled alive out of the mangle and reached salvation.

The Gunpower Plot

THE chief weakness of those who have attacked the traditional story of the Gunpowder Plot has been their inability to supply a reasonable alternative. One effect of this—and it is another weakness in itself—has been a tendency to launch attacks against every point that seemed at all vulnerable, with the result that frequently lines of argument have become entangled, not to say mutually destructive. In particular, if it is being argued that the plot was known to the Government from the beginning it is confusing to bring in another argument that there was really no plot at all. Unless, of course, it is made clear that there were two plots, one devised by the conspirators, and another that was foisted on them at the last moment by the Government. But that is a position difficult to maintain without the help of a firm alternative hypothesis. What is true in this instance is true in general. The traditional story is hallowed by time, and to that extent has proved itself a coherent and durable affair. As long as it is not *entirely* demolished (which so far it has not been), the historian is perfectly entitled to maintain it—until a more coherent and more strictly factual alternative is offered in its place. As an example one may take what was probably the strongest part of S. R. Gardiner's famous defence of the traditional story:[1] the chapter in which he claims to show that the series of Fawkes's elicited confessions build themselves up into the most likely outline of what really happened. Fawkes appears to have confessed gradually, as one would expect; by the time he had finished there is an outline whose psychological probability is enough to satisfy anyone who is already swayed that way by traditional authority. There is at least the basis of a story which no merely

[1] *What the Gunpowder Plot was.*

destructive criticism can hope to rival. In short, any sort of house, however battered and holed, is preferable to a howling wilderness of doubt.

The Catholic apologist, if anyone, should be able to sympathise with this position; for he has frequently himself had to hang on to a traditional story in the teeth of the most frightful gales of scepticism, only to find in the end that the gales have died away and the house is still standing—though perhaps in need of some minor alterations. During the storm, his last argument, when all else may have seemed lost, has always been: "There is no reasonable alternative."

Before suggesting a reasonable alternative to the traditional story, it is necessary to decide impartially what bits of it should definitely be rejected. Now that the dust of the most recent controversy has settled, it seems possible to do this at once briefly and impartially. So many points have been argued with such skill and thoroughness on both sides that it should now be possible, without too much detail, to separate those bits of the traditional story which have been completely undermined or seriously damaged from those that remain intact or only scratched. This is not a merely demolitional process. Men's actions have this about them: that when one version is proved false, another more probable version automatically suggests itself. This would seem to be a reason for disputing Fr Gerard's conclusion that the true history of the plot can now be known to no man. Surely, if a sufficient number of bits (men's actions) are removed from the traditional story, a sufficient number of alternatives should suggest themselves, so that we may judge whether they supply an outline sufficiently coherent and probable to displace the original. A third possibility may be that the traditional story has not to be abolished but only repaired and perhaps altered in parts.

As a modest beginning let us take the strongest part of the traditional story: Fawkes's confessions. There are several flaws in them, but here we may be content to fix on two: one unwarranted insertion, and one contradiction. The insertion is in the *King's Book* copy of Fawkes's confession of 17 November, where there is a parenthesis that incriminates

Hugh Owen. But this parenthesis is not in the written copy of the confession. In this point, then, the traditional story breaks down. It is true that this also supplies a possible argument for its truth as a whole, because, where there is a false insertion, it is natural to suppose that the closing passages are true. On the other hand it invites one to be cautious.

The second flaw, the contradiction, concerns the names of the seven principal conspirators who were more deeply involved than the remaining five. On two occasions, 8 and 17 November, Fawkes is quoted as accusing Robert Winter as being the seventh conspirator. Yet, on 28 November, Coke —in a private note which must be believed, for it was for his own satisfaction—wrote that no one had yet accused R. Winter. In other words, Fawkes did not make the statement attributed to him in public by the Government. The matter is complicated because in the original copy of the 8th Winter's name has been substituted, whereas in the original copy of the 17th it has been erased. Gardiner, after some very ingenious attempts to utilise these erasures, is content to fall back on the plea that the Government made a mistake. This might explain one of the alterations, but not both; nor does it explain why Coke, who was altogether in the Government's confidence, should not have accepted the Government's version.

The inference is inevitable: that Fawkes did not have an altogether clear idea of what he was being called on to sign. This is a very natural likelihood, if one recalls the circumstances. By the 8th he was *in extremis* so weak with pain that, apparently, he could not complete his signature. It must also be remarked that in these two crucial confessions, that of the 8th and that of the 17th—which is supposed to be simply an amplification of the earlier one—Fawkes's signature and those of the examining peers are not present; all that survives is a written copy with the names written in by the copyist. There must, argues Gardiner, have been a signed original which is now lost. It is a natural presumption, not unsatisfactory in itself, but it does not satisfy the earlier doubt. There remains a twofold and not unjustifiable suspicion: that Fawkes was

143

not capable of scrutinising *all* that he was supposed to have said and was being forced to sign: and that the Government was capable of making insertions and alterations, even after he had signed it.

Gardiner clearly felt the force of this doubt, for he argued that Fawkes's confessions could not be *all* fabricated (no one had yet asserted this) for there were passages—such as Fawkes's exculpation of Gerard—which the Government would not possibly have invented. This is perfectly true—though it also suggests that what the Government wanted from Fawkes was not so much his own statements as his consent to theirs; he would never have mentioned Gerard's name unless it had been first mentioned to him. The opposition case is that there is no guarantee that false assertions were not worked into the genuine fabric of Fawkes's confessions: either by erasions and alterations after he had signed, or by incapacitating him before he signed. Gardiner, however, was perfectly right in replying that the actual evidence—of erasions and alterations—is not formidable; it does not affect the main story, and it is insufficient of itself to impugn the Government's good faith. Gardiner's case is actually strengthened by a frank admission that, by our legal standards, Jacobean methods were brutal and unscrupulous—especially in the case of a determined and dangerous victim like Fawkes. As long as they were satisfied that he was guilty in the main, they felt quite justified in filling in the details themselves.

But Gardiner goes too far when he claims that Fawkes's confessions are an insuperable obstacle to the opponents of the traditional story. The most one can say is that Fawkes's confessions should stand firm—as long as the supporting confessions around them are not undermined; that the Government's rough-and-ready good faith should be assumed —unless very much more serious evidence is brought against it.

Evidence of this nature is, however, not lacking. It remains to be seen how serious it is.

There is the matter of Bates's confession. Government fabrication in this case, if the opposition view is accepted, goes far beyond the rough-and-ready improvisation that was justified by the times. Bates is reported as confessing (again the original is not extant) on 4 December: that he had believed the plot to be sinful; that Catesby, his master, and Thomas Wintour forced him to ask the Jesuit Tesimond about it in confession; *that the Jesuit told him to go ahead and have no scruples;* and that Catesby and Wintour then obliged him to pledge his secrecy by taking the Sacrament. This should have been a perfect confession from Salisbury's point of view, for he was above all anxious to incriminate the Jesuits. It is strange, therefore, that in his despatches after this date he does not seem satisfied that any priest has yet been sufficiently implicated. Stranger still, perhaps, is the absence of any evidence that Thomas Wintour was ever confronted with this most damning document. When Thomas Wintour denied the complicity of any priest, no one seems to have said to him: "You liar! Look what Bates has deposed against you." Presumably Thomas Wintour, a brave and devout Catholic (and therefore unlikely to have committed the sacrilege here alleged) would have replied, "It is you who are the liars. This is false, and Bates could not have said it unless he was tortured beyond recognition." Bates's confession seems never to have been used against the conspirators except by Coke at the trial in a vague and rhetorical manner which would have been impossible to answer. It was used in the same manner against Garnet, but not pressed, because by that time the Government had by eavesdropping discovered an admission by Garnet which ran quite counter to Bates's. Garnet revealed that Tesimond, having first heard *from Catesby* in confession about the plot (just *what* plot is not clear) and having denounced it as grievously sinful, was allowed by Catesby *sub sigillo confessionis* to reveal the matter to Garnet. This clearly contradicts Bates's confession which alleges that Tesimond gave the plot his blessing.

What should reasonably be taken as deciding the matter is that Tesimond afterwards deposed on his word as a priest that he had never in any way approved of the plot that the Government discovered. A fair verdict must be that the substance of Bates's confession was false. It was, therefore, either forced on him by torture, or fabricated by a Government employee. Bates's subsequent behaviour makes the latter alternative much more likely: he remained loyal and constant till his death, remorseful over some very minor breach of confidence, but apparently quite oblivious of this major and devastating betrayal of his code.

Once again it must be said that the falsity of Bates's confession does not directly touch the main story of the plot—the mine, the cellar, and so forth. But the implication of it is disquieting. It is no longer possible to assume the good faith of the Government, even according to rough and ready standards of justice. The arguments against Fawkes's confessions thus gain in proportion; and others, not mentioned before, now acquire a right to be heard. For example, on 9 November Fawkes is said to have revealed the story of the mine. Yet in a report sent off on the 9th, describing the progress of the investigation, Salisbury made no mention of this sensational discovery. It is perfectly possible that the dispatch was sent off before the discovery was made. But falsehood in one part of a story breeds suspicion in others.

So far there has been no question of forgery. Fawkes's confessions were not written in his own hand; they were written by a clerk and presented to Fawkes to sign. Moreover, as has been stated in several cases his signature also is not in his own hand, but in that of the copyist. The Government's good faith, it was said, was the guarantee for the presumption that there was a signed original now lost. The same is true of Bates's confession, of which there is no trace of the signed original. In this case the presumption of the Government's good faith cannot be granted. But in neither case are there grounds to suspect forgery.

We now come to incontrovertible evidence that forgery *was* made use of in the investigations leading up to the trial. The proof is in the intercepted correspondence between Fr Garnet and Anne Vaux when Garnet was in prison. They exchanged letters written in orange-juice which remained invisible until the paper was warmed. The Government anxious for incriminating details, intercepted nearly all this correspondence. Naturally the letters once the writing had been made visible by warming them, could no longer be passed on to the correspondents as if they had not been intercepted. Yet the two continued to correspond, and the originals continued to come into Government hands where they remained. The only possible conclusion is that what the correspondents actually received were copies so expertly forged as to deceive their own close knowledge of each other's handwriting. There is no escaping this evidence.

Now, in Garnet's crucial confession of 8 March there is an awkward and improbable parenthesis that incriminates Hugh Owen in just the same way as the false parenthesis in Fawkes's confession. By the ordinary rule of textual criticism Garnet's parenthesis is open to grave doubt. Yet the whole of the confession in which it occurs purports to be in his own handwriting; there is no question of insertion by another hand. It has just been proved that there was a forger available who could counterfeit Garnet's writing to perfection. The inference is that the whole confession is in a forger's hand. That does not mean that none of the confession includes his own words: the parenthesis rather suggests that the enclosing sentence *was* in his own words. But it means that, while some parts of the confession may be in his own words, others are certainly not. Re-copying in a forged hand on such a lavish scale would not be done without a sufficient purpose.

Against this background we come to the confession of Thomas Wintour. Here the reasons for and against forgery have been fully set out in *The Month* (January–May 1952) in the controversy between Mr Hugh Ross Williamson and Dr and Mrs Jenkins. The result was in favour of Ross Williamson's lucid and patient exposition. The Hatfield draft (if it is a draft) which appears to be in Wintour's handwriting does not carry conviction as really being so. Although the handwriting (as in the case of Garnet) is indistinguishable from Wintour's normal style, yet its fluency, increasing as the long letter goes on, is in marked contrast to a genuine fragment written by him at the same time in the unsteady hand of a wounded man. Further, some at least of the marginal additions, in small delicate letters, appear to have been added *after* the document passed out of his hands into those of his prosecutors. Moreover, his signature, though the forger would not have been in a position to know this—is not the same as in any of the other eight instances of it that are known to exist. Finally the attestation of the examining peers, supposed to have been added to the original, are not present; and the defence is obliged to conjecture—with S. R. Gardiner —that there was *another finished version* in Wintour's handwriting in which they were present. The argument here, which is a plausible one—is that Wintour was ordered to re-write the whole thing incorporating the marginal additions in the text. He may have been but there is absolutely no evidence that he did. The objections therefore, to the authenticity of this Hatfield draft remain very formidable. Much more might—and has been—said on either side; and there can be no absolute certainty either way, but the probability would seem to be the same as in Garnet's confession of 8 March: namely that large tracts of the confession may well be in Wintour's own words, but that the whole was re-written by an expert forger with such additions and insertions as the prosecution desired. Nor is there anything outrageous in this suggestion since two brilliant forgers, Phelippes and Barnes, who were often employed in this sort of work, were certainly to hand at that moment, and Phelippes was actually plying his trade in 1605.

The question of Wintour's confession is decisive in this sense only, that its authenticity or the reverse may be said to tip the scale either for or against the general reliability of the traditional story. One might pass over the small addition to Fawkes's confession as being an excusable lapse with no implication of forgery, and one might rebut the probability that there was the same sort of insertion in Garnet's confession of 8 March, thus escaping the conclusion that the whole is in a forger's hand. But if one admits the probability that Wintour's confession is in a forged hand, then the dyke is finally opened to a flood of doubt. One must again recall: (*a*) that Fawkes's crucial confessions were either not actually signed by him, or presented to him when he was barely strong enough to sign them; (*b*) that almost certainly, Bates's confession was a fabrication; (*c*) that with complete certainty, there was wholesale forgery of Garnet's correspondence in prison. The question follows—Is ANY of the traditional story worth believing?

"Flood of doubt" is an emotive phrase; and, willy-nilly, this is the time when some sort of sympathy or antipathy is almost bound to appear. And quite rightly. Sympathy with the chivalrous character of the recusant gentlemen has its place as an argument in their favour. On the other hand there is a very sound sort of sentiment that refuses to abandon an old traditional position until absolutely forced to. The defence can refuse to accept a vague global doubt; it can meet each objection separately and dismiss it either as unproved or, if proved as irrelevant. This is a perfectly honourable method of argument and one much used by theologians to defend their tenets in the days when "science" seemed to have all the answers.

The single-minded inquirer, however, must resist both these extremes. He has found enough to make him seriously question the traditional story, but by no means enough to make him definitely disbelieve it. The only thing for him is to go on inquiring.

Leaving for the present the question of forgery, there are several other statements in the traditional story which do not bear the stamp of truth. There is what S. R. Gardiner condescended to call "the little comedy at Hoxton"—that is the warning letter to Lord Monteagle—and several other connected features all pointing to the same conclusion: the conclusion that Salisbury knew of the plot beforehand, and staged his own methods of bringing it to light in the most dramatic manner. To insist on this would be rather like flogging a dead horse. Salisbury himself admitted—and the admission itself is too obvious to need further confirmation— that the recusants in question were marked men, and that he was expecting them to cause trouble timed for the opening of Parliament. There is no need to press this point any further. On paper, Salisbury's pre-knowledge is not incompatible with the substance of his story being true. But in reality, if one thinks oneself back into the actual situation, it opens up an objection to the traditional story far more formidable than any yet encountered. This objection, instead of nibbling piecemeal at the plot's credibility, as the arguments for forgery do, undermines the whole fabric of it. Let it be examined, generously, therefore, but with an interior caution.

Consider the situation from two points of view. First from the point of view of Catesby and his friends. After the letter to Monteagle, they knew that they were being watched, that they were suspected of planning a deadly blow for the opening of Parliament, that Percy's house a few feet from the Parliament House would be an object of especial suspicion, that there would be extra precautions taken on the eve of the 5th. They must have known that there was not one chance in a million that their enormous deposit of gunpowder would pass undetected, and not one chance in ten million that Fawkes would be left in peace to lay his train for midday on the 5th. Yet they continued to haunt the scene of their abortive crime. The Chamberlain going his rounds with extra vigilance—as they knew he must do—noted the piled up wood in the vault and noted Fawkes standing by. And still they did nothing. They did not even try to blow the place up empty —which was the most sensible way of using the powder, as well as a good symbolic gesture. But it is not worth amplifying the point further. It is a simple one. You either see it or you don't. All the historians have seen it to the point of exclaiming: *"They were mad!"* But *were* they? There was no panic or frenzy. The movements of Fawkes, Catesby and the rest were cold and deliberate. They were possessed, if anything, by a bleared, brutish, inhuman stupidity. Possessed by the Devil, in fact. Bewitched like Circe's swine. That, of course is what the Government Book wanted their readers to believe, and knew that in the prevailing atmosphere they would have no difficulty in doing so. If an incredible thing really happens, it must be believed. But here is where the question of forgery and fabrication returns. Supposing you are asked to believe an incredible thing on the sole authority of people whose creditability you have serious reasons to doubt? That is a very different question, and that is the position in which the single-minded inquirer is now asked to find himself (but he is not to be stampeded).

Let us suppose that the conspirators were lunatics during the period in question (though they were clearly not so either before or after). But was Salisbury mad too? Look at it from his point of view, that is, from his alleged point of view. It is now virtually admitted by all, that the Monteagle letter was either staged by him or with his foreknowledge. He knew that there was a vast deposit of gunpowder somewhere near Percy's house, and that there was a lunatic at large (by his own account) ready to set it off at any moment. Would any sane man—let alone the virtual head of a Government—have allowed that period, especially those last six hours, to elapse before doing anything. Fawkes had perfect freedom during those last six hours. It was touch and go that he would blow the place up there and then. Empty, of course. But Salisbury could not possibly take that risk. It would have been an appalling and inexcusable blot upon his vigilance. It would have been a sort of portent that would have shaken everybody's confidence in the Government. Indeed, to have blown it up empty would have been a triumph for the conspirators —an I.R.A. man's dream of final glory. Salisbury would never have taken that risk. Once again it must be emphasised, this is not a question of cut-and-dried argument. It is a question of being able to swallow a monstrous psychological improbability, or not being able to. And here again the arguments for forgery take their place. Is it right to swallow such a story when it is only proferred on such tarnished evidence?

Hitherto the arguments for Salisbury's fore-knowledge have been used to prove his unscrupulous cunning. That is a superfluous line of argument. The fact is that they prove him guilty of crazy, slap-happy, suicidal recklessness. By a stretch of the imagination it is possible to believe that the conspirators were lunatics. But it is not possible to believe that Salisbury was a lunatic.

It is not now a question of doubting this or that detail of the Government story. It is a question of asking straight out —WAS THERE ANY GUNPOWDER THERE AT ALL?

Once that cat is out of the bag, it is surprising how well it runs. How did the conspirators—marked men and closely watched—get hold of their enormous supplies? Equally inexplicable—as the problem—of how they got it—is the question why the Government never inquired how they got it. They have acquired two tons of the stuff, either shipped in from abroad, or stolen from the Government's arsenals under its very nose. Nothing like it has been heard of before or since. Any normal Government would be hopping with anxiety to know how it was done. Yet from this most vigilant Government there is not a question, not the hint of a question, in any of the confessions.

Instead, there are a couple of letters which now assume a very sinister significance. One dated 27 November is from the Keeper of the Arsenal to Salisbury. The King, he says, wants to know why, when powder was delivered at Lambeth "by the porters" (*whose* porters?) it was received by a beardless young man who did not answer to the description of the conspirator supposed to be concerned—or indeed to any of the conspirators who were all bearded. This opens up another breach in the traditional story, but it must be relegated to a footnote. The point at present is that in spite of a further suggestion by the King that the delivery of the powder should be inquired into, there was no such inquiry. There was the exact reverse. There is another letter of a much later date—a letter strongly suggestive of blackmail—which reveals that the records of the intake and delivery during the crucial period 1604-6 were not allowed to be seen by an official auditor. Something that is really credible is here beginning to take shape; but, naturally, its full shape is only confused by conjecture about details of which we can know nothing. All that can be said is that there are grounds for a suggestion that the only powder in the plot was used by the real framers of the plot to convince some actual eye-witnesses that gunpowder was involved.

Here it is worth mentioning the report of the member of the French Embassy, written the day after Fawkes's arrest, that the only powder discovered was a single small keg—and that, not in the vault under Parliament but in *Percy's house*. It is easy to dismiss this report as a by-blow of Gallic scepticism, or alternatively of Gallic credulity. But at least it is credible. The disappearance of two tons into thin air is not.

And here it may be said that—contrary to Gardiner's claim —there can be traced an early and consistent tradition of disbelief in the Gunpowder Plot.

But here the single-minded inquirer must intervene before the "flood of doubt" becomes an ocean of suggestions. The psychological argument—the "madness" of the conspirators and of Salisbury—cannot be decisive. You can never be sure how people will behave in varying circumstances. Besides, Salisbury may have taken precautions which, of course he would not mention, but which need not affect the main substance of his story. Against the psychological argument, one who wished to adhere to the last to the traditional story may have to make a tactical retreat at certain points, but he can still remain entrenched in the central citadel without his integrity being impugned.

The absence of inquiry into the acquisition of the gunpowder is, however, in a different category. But before going on to that, the single-minded inquirer would like to draw what seems to him a legitimate inference from the strange behaviour of Salisbury and the conspirators in the days preceding the 5th. It is not an inference which visibly helps either a traditional or a radical answer to the problem; it remains suspended in mid-air. But it is an inference that one can make with the feeling that one is on solid ground and not on the shifting sands of conjecture. If we accept the Monteagle letter as officially inspired, then it is clear that some official personage was trying to disperse the conspirators, to send them out of London and possibly abroad; and it seems equally clear that the conspirators were obstinately refusing to take their chance of escape. No further inference can be drawn as to the motives of either party; but that so far as it goes seems to be a contribution towards the truth wherever it may lie. It is a clue if only one knew how to interpret it.

But to return to the matter of the conspirators' two tons of gunpowder. *How did they get it? and where did it go to?* The unwillingness of the Government to answer these questions is perhaps, of all the objections, the ugliest and most formidable yet brought against the traditional story. There is no getting away from the inference that the Government had something to hide. There seems to be room for only two possible explanations. Either: gunpowder was issued to the conspirators with the connivance of the authorities. Or: the conspirators never had two tons of gunpowder under the Parliament house. The single-minded inquirer will probably consider both these explanations too far-fetched unless they are supported by more solid evidence than has yet been produced. The only thing he can do for the moment is to shelve the question. Nevertheless it remains an ugly thorn in the mind: "How did they get it and where did it go to?"

Is there any other evidence that strikes at the centre—not merely the periphery—of the Government story? There is the matter of the mine.

Fr Gerard in his book[1] devoted a good deal of space to the physical unlikelihood that these inexpert diggers could have avoided detection in a not unfrequented area: the noise of their operations, and the disposal of enormous quantities of earth and huge stones (the river with its wide fringe of ooze, was not such a good dumping place as Gardiner, in his answer to Gerard, seemed to think). But there are other obstacles to the mine story which are easier for us to assess. They had not the faintest hope of reaching the required spot in February when Parliament was first due; and they had not the faintest reason to believe that the King, let alone his heir, or if Lord Salisbury would be present; the King very rarely attended and Salisbury did, in fact, arrange to be absent on the 5th. It is possible of course that they believed Divine Providence would arrange all for them. But belief in Divine Providence will not account for the plain stupidity of the next difficulty; that they did not realise till they heard "the rushing of coals" over their heads that there was a vault or cellar a few feet from their house—and *annexed to it*—which would have saved them all their futile and herculean labours. We are asked to believe that, having hired a house and taken stock of the surroundings, it took them nine months to realise that a vault immediately under Parliament House might be the most convenient place from which to blow up Parliament House. It is asking a lot.

[1] *What was the Gunpowder Plot?*

It is now time to enumerate those parts of the traditional story which can honestly be rejected as false, and to see whether the gaps left by their rejection suggest a coherent alternative.

First of all, and principally, both the mine and the thirty-six barrels of gunpowder must go. At the same time the notion of some gunpowder must remain, because it is the best explanation of a piece of evidence which must be accepted—namely Catesby's case-of-conscience to Garnet about some innocent suffering with the guilty. There is also another piece of evidence that has now a good claim to be accepted; it is the early report from the French embassy that one keg of powder was discovered beneath the Painted Chamber. This makes sense. A small barrel is as much as the conspirators could possibly have collected by private means. The notion of the Painted Chamber, while excluding much absurdity, is also supported by another piece of evidence which was previously mentioned as a difficulty: the detail that Knyvet arrested Fawkes by entering the Vault "by another door", i.e., obviously by a door from *inside* the Parliament House. There is nothing absurd about this detail but it involves the absurdity that the Vault was always liable to visits from a parliamentary official. But if the scene of the crime was to be the Painted Chamber, not the vault, this door becomes an asset, not a difficulty. It provides a means whereby a single barrel, in the form of a petard or bomb, could be brought from the Percy House to beneath the Painted Chamber *via* the Vault, and, once brought, hidden securely by a skilled engineer.

The next absurdity that must go with the previous one, is the idea of the conspirators waiting passively for a week or ten days while their thirty-six barrels pleaded for discovery. If there was only one bomb and that hidden securely in a place not yet apparently suspected, there was still a sporting chance of getting away with it. What before in the conspirators appeared so improbably as brutish stupidity now becomes what they really possessed—nerves of steel. The more so if one excludes the necessity of any particular date as the deadline. This last reflection follows from the choice of the

Painted Chamber. It was not the whole House in its session that was aimed it, the objective was the more active part of the Privy Council at any time, before or during the session, when they gathered together in the Painted Chamber. Among them, and their attendants there were a sufficient number of relatively honest men to provide Catesby with his scruples.

Another absurdity in the official story that now drops off of itself is that the conspirators aimed at exterminating the King and the Royal Family, whom they had no reason to think would be present in Parliament. On the other hand the notion of kidnapping the Royal Family, though it presents difficulties, cannot be rejected. It is in keeping, and, moreover it is supported by evidence not emanating from the Government.

The letters of Sir Everard Digby, written apparently from prison to his wife, and discovered by his son half a century later, are so guarded as to be obscure: nevertheless they shed some rays of light. They show him as by no means Catesby's half-hearted dupe, but as one of the leaders convinced that the undertaking was a noble and chivalrous one, and amazed that his fellow-Catholics are crying out against him. Taking this in conjunction with the known character and ideals of Sir Everard, it is a powerful argument that the plot he was engaged in, Catesby's plot, was not the plot that the Government claimed to have discovered. But apart from that there are some details pointing to the same conclusion.

He is trying to explain to his wife and through her to others, that his conscience is clear. He refers to the most questionable part of the plot as the attempt to "hurt my Lord Salisbury"—presumably a meiosis but it cannot be taken as signifying a general massacre—for blowing him up. Another passage makes it still clearer that the King was not involved. Catesby, he says, was going to proclaim Prince *Charles* the Heir Apparent on his way out of London. Something was evidently going to happen to Prince *Henry*; but the King was still to be King, and Charles his heir. Princess Elizabeth was also to be carried off, and that was to be Digby's special care. Right up to the 5th, he had alternative plans depending on whether she should be in Rutland or

Warwickshire. This makes it clear that the 5th was *not* considered as a deadline for the carrying out of the plot. That fact, small though it is, is a most important clue: for the date of the 5th is a sort of lynch-pin in the official story. Once it is removed the official story begins to fall apart and make room for the real plot which the conspirators were planning.

Several parts of the real plot are already apparent. But clearly a vital clue is missing, which, if we had it would give life and purpose to the parts. Digby hints plainly at this missing clue but does not name it. "If this design had taken place, there could have been no doubt of other success." The design he is talking about is evidently connected with the blowing-up of the Privy Council. But there must have been a twist to it which now evades us.

We can discern the outline of a plot much more credible—and more credibly attested—than the official one. But until that final element is discovered, its presentation will lack conviction; and the official story will still continue to hold the field—at least among those who follow Tertullian's maxim—*Credo quia impossibile.*

157